"Robby Dawkins' bo[...] aging and edifying for those who want to be strong and effective in the Lord's service. I encourage its reading and putting into practice its teachings. It challenges us to believe who we really are and to act accordingly."

Dr. Randy Clark, founder, Apostolic Network of Global Awakening

"Robby has hit the nail on the head with this book! The plans God has for our lives are worth fighting for. And fighting is what we need to be prepared to do. To know your enemy is a plan for every mighty warrior. I encourage every believer to get familiar with this book and put its truth into practice. Now is the time to rise up to our true identity in Christ."

Major Danielle Strickland, The Salvation Army

"*Identity Thief* is an honest, vulnerable, open, faith-filled, big-hearted and encouraging book. In other words, exactly like its author. I commend both the book and its author to you."

Mike Pilavachi, Soul Survivor

"Robby Dawkins' *Identity Thief* is honest, real and thought-provoking. Being Christian often means giving up on winning popularity contests. Could it be that our false sense of humility and the lies of the enemy have left us unbranded, without distinction and ultimately without any form of identity? Robby's honest tell-all of finding his identity shows how God will replace the death caused by religion with the life Christ invokes. This book is both a testimony and a celebration of knowing who we are in Christ, resting in our purpose and relentlessly pursuing God's unique call on our lives."

Leon Schoeman, network and content director, TBN UK and TBN Europe

"Following Jesus was never meant to be boring! In this book we capture afresh the impact of the love, grace and power of Jesus, and the way in which it produces transformed lives."

Mark Bailey, national leader, New Wine England

"Robby Dawkins is a gift to the Church and a danger to the devil. Each time I hear him speak or read his words, I come away challenged to be more relentless in love and courageous in power. His book *Identity Thief* clearly communicates the fact that both power and love are not things we do, but who we are, because it is who our Father is. After reading *Identity Thief*, not only will you know Robby Dawkins better, but you will know who the Father created you to be, a gift to the world and a danger to darkness."

Bob Hazlett, author, *Think Like Heaven: Change Your Thinking, Change Your World*

IDENTITY **THIEF**

IDENTITY **THIEF**

EXPOSING SATAN'S PLAN TO STEAL YOUR
PURPOSE, PASSION AND POWER

ROBBY DAWKINS

Chosen

a division of Baker Publishing Group
Minneapolis, Minnesota

Published by Chosen Books
11400 Hampshire Avenue South
Bloomington, Minnesota 55438
www.chosenbooks.com

Chosen Books is a division of
Baker Publishing Group, Grand Rapids, Michigan

Printed in the United States of America

Library of Congress Cataloging-in-Publication Data
Dawkins, Robby.
    Identity thief : exposing Satan's plan to steal your purpose, passion, and power / Robby Dawkins.
       pages cm
    Summary: "Have you unintentionally put limits on God's power? Discover who you truly are in Christ, and reclaim the identity that Satan is trying to steal away"—Provided by publisher.
      ISBN 978-0-8007-9778-2 (pbk. : alk. paper)
      1. Identity (Psychology)—Religious aspects—Christianity. 2. Devil—Christianity. 3. Spiritual warfare. I. Title.
    BV4509.5.D293 2015
    248.4—dc23   2015024696

Cover design by Gearbox

17 18 19 20 21   7 6 5 4 3 2

I dedicate this book to my six sons, Judah, Micah, Isaiah, Elijah, Canah and Caspian. I wrote this book for you and have allowed the world to listen in on our conversation. You are six young lions into whom your mother and I have poured everything we have and are. We know your identities are formed to turn the world upside down for our great King. As you wage war against the Identity Thief, may you know your father and mother are in the stands, cheering you six champions on to amazing victory. We love you and salute you. For the Kingdom!

CONTENTS

FOREWORD

I first met Robby Dawkins this year when I interviewed him for my television show, *It's Supernatural!* He impressed me because his passion was not "Look at how God uses me," but instead "Everything I can do, you can do, too. And I want to mentor you to go farther than I have."

Even if you have never moved in supernatural gifting and healing, spend a week with Robby in the streets and you will prophesy, pray for and see the sick healed and lead people to Jesus. How refreshing! In other words, you will be normal—normal as defined by the Bible.

Most believers have never understood and walked in their true identity. As a result, they have never walked into their full destiny. But if not now, when? God has a specific job and destiny for your life. No one can do it as well as you. God does not make junk. You are His workmanship. But the Identity Thief has tampered with your true identity.

This book will give you the course correction to embrace your true destiny. It is not too late. It is time to get out of the boat and walk on water. Why stay in the boat? It is time to be normal and to be naturally supernatural.

Sid Roth, host, *It's Supernatural!*

1

WE'VE BEEN HACKED!

"The thief comes only to steal and kill and destroy; I have come that they may have life, and have it to the full."

John 10:10

Trent seemed like an ordinary guy.

He was generally good-looking, but nothing about him made him stand out in a crowd. He was of average height, build and complexion. He was one of those people who look vaguely familiar. When I met him for the first time, I had a feeling I had met him somewhere before.

But I knew that had not happened, because Trent had spent nine years in prison before he began attending the church I pastored.

His fiancée, Rachel, a lovely young lady who was a committed Christian, started coming to our church before he did. He had actually written me a letter from prison, saying she was the best thing that had ever happened to him and that he was going to start coming to church with her as soon as he was paroled. He did not mention anything about why he was serving time, and when I asked his future wife about it, she said, "I'd rather let him tell you about that."

Trent was true to his word. He was released from prison within a month or two of writing that letter, and he began attending church faithfully.

I liked him immediately. He was outgoing, obviously loved the Lord and was ready to serve wherever we needed him.

In fact, the more I got to know Trent, the more I was puzzled to think he could have done anything that would result in nine years behind bars. I felt knowing about his life would help me be a better pastor to him. Were there particular struggles I could help him deal with? Any special guidance I could give him?

So one day I invited him out for coffee and told him I would like to know more about him.

He stared off into space for a minute and then asked, "Robby, when you were a boy, did your dad ever play ball with you?"

I shook my head. "Not really. My dad was more of a communicator. We talked a lot—about everything. But we did play catch sometimes."

He said, "Well, some dads teach their kids how to play ball or how to have a good conversation. My dad taught me how to steal. My parents would take me into jewelry stores, and they'd distract the clerk so I could grab a handful of jewelry and stuff it in my pocket. My dad taught me how to cheat. He taught me how to lie. That was the family trait."

I am almost never at a loss for words. But at that moment, all I could think to say was, "I'm so sorry."

A shadow moved across Trent's face as he relived his painful childhood memories. "I also learned to fight when I was very young," he continued. "My dad said he wanted to make sure I could hold my own. Sometimes he'd start fistfights with me. That's the way my life was until I finished high school and took off on my own. Then I found a better way to steal."

"What was that?"

"I learned how to get people's personal information from things they threw away. I got imprints from their credit cards. I even befriended people just so I could use the stuff they told me—things like their mother's maiden name, where they went to school, anything I might use to impersonate them. I would use people until they were on the brink of ruin or even *in* ruin, and then I moved on to the next person."

He looked at me and said, "Robby, I'm an identity thief."

As a man who pastored for more than two decades, I have heard a lot of confessions. I have had people come up to me and confess murders that have gone unpunished. I have had husbands and wives confess affairs, and I have had wives share that their husbands did not know a child was not theirs. I have had men tell me they were living dual lives—that they had a wife and family at home but were hanging out in gay bars. As far as I can remember, though, that was the first time I had ever heard the term *identity thief*.

It certainly was not the last. Today, it seems we are living in the age of identity theft. Millions of us have had our bank, credit card accounts or social media accounts hacked. If you send and receive emails, then you have almost certainly received a number of "phishing" emails that try to trick you into giving your social security number or other personal information. Identity thieves call us on the telephone, saying that we owe back taxes and that the IRS wants us to pay them right now via credit card. I do not have to tell you, because you already know: Identity thieves are everywhere!

In 2012, people like Trent stole more than $21 billion from their unsuspecting victims,[1] and the number is growing fast. Identity theft is the fastest-growing crime in the world.[2]

Even as I was in the process of writing this book, computer hackers stole the personal data of millions of customers of the huge insurance company Anthem Blue Cross. According to news reports, the thieves procured information—like the names, birthdays, social security numbers, addresses and much more—of up to eighty million Anthem customers.[3] It is, up until now, the largest data breach in corporate history. I say "up until now" because it probably will not be long until something even worse happens.

We are all at risk.

If you are like me, it frightens you to think that someone with criminal intentions has access to all of your personal information. It is a horrible feeling to be used and violated in this way. It is like coming home at the end of the day to discover burglars have ransacked your house and taken many of your most cherished items. Identity thieves are everywhere, and that is why it is important to do everything you possibly can to protect yourself from them.

The Original Identity Thief

But there is an Identity Thief who steals much more than material things like social security numbers, credit cards and cash. It is one thing when someone takes over your various accounts and operates as you, but this Thief does one worse:

He convinces you that you are someone other than who you really are.

More than likely, he has already done so.

The thieves that hacked into Anthem got the personal information of eighty million people. But there are more than seven billion people on this planet, and the Thief I am talking about has the goods on all of us. He knows every password. Every PIN. He knows your social security number, your mom's maiden name—everything.

Even worse, he knows where each one of us is vulnerable to spiritual attack. He knows how to make us Christians feel small and miserable when, in fact, we are heirs of our Father God. He gets us to give up on God and ourselves by convincing us we are disqualified. He steals hope and leaves despair. He destroys faith with unbelief and levels hope with fear.

Of course, I am talking about our enemy—Satan. He is trying to steal our identity and leave us powerless. He is trying to rob us of the rights that are ours as children of God.

But there is good news, and that is why I am writing this book.

If you belong to Jesus, then you are a child of God. You have the right to walk in power and victory and to expect miraculous answers to your prayers. Knowing your identity and position in Christ is the essential truth that will set you free to enter into the unimaginable realm of life in God that is your birthright and to operate in the power and authority Christ came to reinstate for you.

That is what this book is meant to teach you. In our journey together in these pages, I will share with you some of the many ways Satan has tried to steal my own identity over the years. I will also show you from personal experience how God can and will enable you to overcome, just as He did for me—and how you can respond when Satan turns and sets his sights on you.

Trent was living the good life as an identity thief. He had plenty of money. In fact, he was so good at what he did that he was recruited by a gang.

But he also had a guilty conscience that would not leave him alone. When he tried covering up his guilt with drugs, he became addicted to heroin and coke. Shortly after that, he slipped up—and wound up in prison.

"I hadn't been in prison too long when Rachel came to see me," he said to me. "She was a Christian, and she told me that God had spoken to her about me and told her to love me unconditionally, because we were going to be married."

Trent says he laughed when she told him this. Rachel did not know who he was or all the things he had done. She did not know what he was capable of doing. How could she promise to love him unconditionally? It was easy to say something like that but a whole lot harder to do. She was a pretty girl, but Trent thought she must be some kind of religious nut.

Even so, day after day, Rachel lived up to her promise. She was kind to Trent. She prayed for him. She assured him she believed in him and knew he could leave his old life behind.

"I'd had a lot of girlfriends," Trent told me, "but none of them had ever treated me the way she did."

Rachel constantly demonstrated the love of God to Trent. And as she did, he found himself falling in love with her.

But then, in telling me the story, Trent shook his head.

"One evening, everything changed," he said. "It was like the light had gone out of her eyes. She told me something terrible had happened. Her mother had found all these charges on her credit card that she hadn't made. She looked me straight in the eye and asked, 'Have you stolen from my mother?'"

For the first time in years, Trent told the truth.

"Yes," he admitted to her.

Her eyes narrowed and grew darker. "Then I want nothing more to do with you!" she cried, turning from him in the prison visitation room and storming out.

Trent stood and watched her go, wanting to call out to her but unable to do so.

"I went back to my cell," he said to me. "It was dark, and it was at night . . . and I just sat there for hours. I couldn't say a word. I couldn't think straight, because all that kept running through my mind was, 'What have I done?'"

Trent said he had never really prayed before that. But finding himself devastated by what he had done to this young woman who had come to mean so much to him, he uttered his first real prayer.

"God, that's the last person on earth I had," he said to God that night, "and she just walked out of my life. Now I'm completely and utterly alone."

Suddenly, Jesus Was There

At that instant, something amazing happened that changed Trent's life forever.

Suddenly, Jesus was with him in his cell, holding out His hand and helping Trent to his feet.

Trent remembers that love radiated out from Christ as He said to Trent, "I want you to come to Me. The life you've been living is not the life I had planned for you. But I will take you and I will change you—and you'll start new."

Trent says the Lord then wrapped His arms around him, and he felt as if he was being swallowed up in light.

"I could feel the warmth coming from Him," he said to me. "He was so real, I could actually smell Him. And I knew something was changing inside of me."

Jesus began telling Trent things about himself—his true identity—that were the exact opposite of the way he had always seen himself.

Jesus said, "You're a truthful man now," but Trent knew he had always been a liar and a thief.

"You're a caring man now," Jesus told him, but Trent knew he had hurt dozens of people without giving their feelings a second thought.

"You are precious to Me," the Lord said, but Trent did not understand how that was possible. Even so, as he stood there in God's embrace, he knew it was all true. He also knew he wanted to be the truthful, caring man God said he was.

When the Lord finally let go of Trent, He simply disappeared.

Trent began to cry out, "Please don't leave me! Please don't go!"

Then, in telling me the story, he said, "I suddenly realized that He hadn't left me. I can't explain it, but I knew He was inside of me."

After That, Everything Changed

The next day, Rachel returned to the prison to see Trent. When he was told he had a visitor, he said, "There must be some mistake. No one wants to see me."

He went to the visiting room and was shocked to find Rachel sitting there. She had a serious look on her face, but she did not look angry, as she had the day before.

"Why are you here?" he asked.

"God spoke to me last night and told me to come back and see you," she replied. "He told me He was changing you at that very moment. He said, 'Forgive him and love him. He has embraced Me.'"

They wept together as Trent shared his life-changing experience from the evening before.

That is when everything changed. Trent had often been placed in isolation for bad behavior, but he became a model prisoner. He decided he was going to be an honest man, no matter what it cost him. As a result of that, in a matter of months, he was moved from a maximum-security prison to a minimum-security facility, where in a short time he was made a trustee. When he proved trustworthy there, he was granted an early release.

As far as Trent was concerned, the best part was experiencing Rachel's forgiveness of him for what he had done. Trent knew he wanted to spend the rest of his life with her, so he got down on his knees and asked her to marry him. He was thrilled when she said yes.

You Are Meant for More

For years, Trent had made his way in life by stealing other people's identities. What he did not know was that Satan had stolen his identity first, from day one. Trent was precious in the sight of God, but Satan had made him feel he was a worthless loser. He was created, as we all are, to shine in a dark world, but instead he had become an instrument of darkness and despair.

And Trent is not the only one.

Let me tell you, for example, about my son Canah. Canah is not a big guy—he is just eleven years old today—but he has a very big heart for people. He loves praying for people and seeing them healed. And you do not have to know Canah very well to realize he is on the autism spectrum.

So, who is Canah? You might describe him as a young autistic kid. And that is just how Satan wants Canah to see himself—by his "imperfections." That is exactly how Satan, the great Identity Thief, wants you to measure yourself, too— as the sum of all your shortcomings and "failures."

But Canah's true identity is this: He is a mighty warrior of God. He is a true friend to everyone who does not have one in the world (as he told me the other day). He is a defender of the weak and a bearer of the Father heart of God.

Here is one way I know this to be true. In August 2013, some of my family went to England for a series of festivals. Canah was there with me, along with my wife, Angie, and our other sons, Judah, Micah, Isaiah, Elijah and Caspian. When I say *festival*, you may think of something with a few hundred people, but these were much bigger events. In that one month, at least fifty thousand people would have attended these New Wine and Soul Survivor festivals. The largest of these meetings had about eleven thousand people in a massive tent, and the smallest had about half that number. GOD TV was there to record on the night I spoke.

At the conclusion of one of those services, more than one thousand people came forward for prayer and healing. Canah had received a word of knowledge about shoulders and hips that needed healing that night.

"Dad, we've done enough talking," he said. "Time to do healing. There are some jacked-up bodies in this place that need to be healed."

Keep in mind that this is a young man who, according to one doctor, would never get to a place where he would look us in the eye or speak. This doctor said Canah had "the worst case of autism" he had ever seen.

But you should have seen Canah on the stage that night. He was pouring out every ounce of his energy to minister healing to people. Two people were immediately and completely healed of severe scoliosis. You could see their posture change right before your eyes. One moment their backs were twisted and bent, and the next they were standing straight and tall. Others were healed that night as well.

God uses Canah to do mighty things, and He can use you, too, despite the lies Satan has been telling you about yourself for all these years.

Do you want to see such miracles? If you belong to Christ, you already have the power you need to see them happen.

Do you want to pray and see the sick healed? You can. Christ is in you. The Holy Spirit is in you. You do not need some deeper revelation or some new experience to bring this to fruition. You just need to begin living the reality of who you are in Christ.

In the pages ahead, we will enter into stories that demonstrate the lifelong battle each of us has been waging with the Identity Thief—sometimes without our even knowing it—and what we can learn about protecting ourselves from his deceit and trickery. As I share my own story and that of others who have given me permission to share theirs, I will teach you how to maintain your identity as an ambassador of Christ and live the courageous adventure God has always intended for you.

Are you ready to live for more?

2

DON'T LISTEN
TO THE LIAR

"He [Satan] was a murderer from the beginning, not holding to the truth, for there is no truth in him. When he lies, he speaks his native language, for he is a liar and the father of lies."

John 8:44

My parents had been serving as missionaries in Japan for a little over a year when my mother became pregnant with me.

About a week after she found out she was pregnant, she was doing laundry in the back room of their house when Satan appeared in the corner. He told her he was Satan, and she believed him because he had appeared out of thin air. He looked like a normal man, but my mother says she could feel the evil and dread that seemed to pour out of him.

As you would expect, she was paralyzed by fear. She described the moment to me years later, saying that "a waterfall of fear" poured over her.

"I Will Kill You and the Baby"

Satan glared at her and growled, "I can't allow this child to be born." If she refused to terminate the pregnancy, he said, "I will kill you and the baby at birth."

Struggling to get the words out, my mother managed to respond, "The Lord clearly has a plan for this child's life that you want to stop, and I will not put my hand against God's plan—even if it means the loss of my own life."

She thought Satan might strike her down on the spot. But instead, he just disappeared. There was no flash of light. No smell of sulfur. He was there, and then he was gone.

My mother did not tell my dad right away what had happened, because she did not want to upset him. But she did not have to tell him. A few days after appearing to her, the devil appeared to my father and made the same threat: If my father allowed me to be born, my mother and I would both die during the birth. My dad pretty much responded the same way my mother had, and again Satan disappeared immediately.

Satan never showed himself to my father again, but my mother says he appeared to her once a month for the rest of her pregnancy, making the same threat over and over. Every time, she responded the same way: She would not put her hand against what God had planned.

Then, near the end of her pregnancy, my mother had a visit from an angel who told her that because she had stayed strong despite Satan's threats, I would be born on Easter Sunday morning—April 10, 1966. The odds of this happening naturally were not great, as my mom's doctor expected me to arrive on March 20. But the angel insisted I would come into the world on Easter Sunday. This would be a sign of God's protection over me and His hand on my life.

The angel did not, however, say a single word about my mother. Her survival was uncertain, but she was not about to back down.

The angel was telling the truth. I was born right on schedule—that is, God's schedule, not man's schedule. When my mother went into labor early that Easter morning, she says she felt she was about to die. But that did not happen. We both survived.

My dad paced the waiting room—as most expectant fathers did in those days—waiting for the obstetrician to come tell him whether he had a son or a daughter and if all had gone well during the delivery. When he saw the doctor approach, he feared the worst. The man was disheveled, and dark rings circled his eyes. He looked as if he had been through an ordeal, and my dad's faith began to waver.

"Congratulations, Reverend Dawkins," the doctor said without the slightest hint of enthusiasm. "You have a healthy baby boy. Your wife and your son are both doing fine."

The doctor then stood there for a moment, and my dad had the feeling he had not said everything he had to say.

"And . . . ?" my dad asked.

"I just left a war zone," the doctor finally offered. "Both mother and child are fine, but it wasn't without a fight."

When my dad pressed him, the doctor could not explain what he meant. Nothing terrible had happened. There was no physical reason why the delivery should have been so hard, but he said every moment felt like a struggle to swim upstream against the current.

You Are Not Who He Says You Are

Satan is one of the most persistent beings God ever created. He never gives up. He was completely defeated when Jesus walked out of the tomb, but he does not seem to realize it. He and his followers never seem to get tired of whispering into the ears of Christ's followers, doing everything within their power to demoralize and defeat us. They constantly try to usher unbelief into our lives and undermine God's Word.

Please believe me when I tell you that you are not the person Satan says you are. You do not have to listen to that condemning voice in your head or those negative feelings in your emotions. Do not trust them. They are his lies. He would like nothing better than to get you to doubt yourself and the God who created you.

Satan loves to hang identities on us that are not who we really are at all. For instance, he likes to call us

Sinner

Disappointment

Failure

Weakling

Doubter

Most of us have been all of these things at one time or another. But they do not define us. They are not who we are. When we accept Jesus Christ as our Lord and Savior, God instead sees us as

Righteous

Achiever

Overcomer

Strong

Faithful

If Satan says you are a sinner, remember that we were *all* sinners, "for all have sinned and fall short of the glory of God" (Romans 3:23). The apostle Paul, who wrote more than half of the New Testament and spread Christianity throughout the known world during the first century, was a man who once persecuted and killed believers. The apostle Peter verbally denied Christ three times. King David committed adultery with another man's wife—and then had him killed to cover up his sin. Talk about sinners! Yet God did great things through each of them, and He plans to do great things through you, as well. All you have to do is believe Him, embrace the identity He gave you at the cross and live that new life He designed for you to live.

Many have referred to God's Kingdom as the upside-down Kingdom. Everything seems to work the opposite of what the world's system says. Remember, this is a Kingdom where love is a weapon of mass destruction against the kingdom of darkness. So are humility, worship, peacemaking and blessing your enemies. If Satan says you are weak, then praise God because of it, for His Word says, "My power is made perfect in weakness" (2 Corinthians 12:9).

If Satan says he is going to destroy you, remember that God is for you. It is just like Paul says:

> If God is for us, who can be against us? He who did not spare his own Son, but gave him up for us all—how will he not also, along with him, graciously give us all things? Who will bring any charge against those whom God has chosen? It is God who justifies. Who then is the one who condemns? No one.
>
> Romans 8:31–34

You Were Created to Reign

I love the way the New Living Translation describes God's words about us during the act of Creation:

> Then God said, "Let us make human beings in our image, to be like us. They will reign . . ."
>
> Genesis 1:26

You were made to reign. Did you know that?

So when Satan is trying to put thoughts in your head of the opposite notion, remember that—and remind him of it, too! Satan can quote Scripture, but he uses it for his own means. He also hates when we quote it back to him. This is because Satan's version of God's Word is always twisted.

Satan has been distorting the Word of God for thousands of years. The first instance is found in the third chapter of Genesis, where he appeared to Adam and Eve in the Garden of Eden. God had told the first man and woman that they could eat the fruit of any tree in the garden except that from the Tree of the Knowledge of Good and Evil.

But when Satan showed up, he asked, "Did God really say, 'You must not eat from any tree in the garden'?" (Genesis 3:1). I can imagine him emphasizing the word *really* and rolling his eyes in a sarcastic way.

When Eve answered by telling him what God had said to them, the devil responded with even more sarcasm. "You won't die," he said, refuting God's Word. "God knows that when you eat from it your eyes will be opened, and you will be like God, knowing good and evil." (See verses 4–5.)

There you have it: the first lie in history.

And Adam and Eve believed it. They already *were* like God, according to Genesis 1:26. So Satan really promised them nothing here.

Even so, they each took a bite of the forbidden fruit, and their eyes were opened.

What happened next? Their eyes were opened and *empowerment* came? No. Their eyes were opened and *joy* came? Again, no. Their eyes were opened and *clarity* came? Not at all.

When their eyes were opened, *shame* came rushing in. They understood for the first time that they were naked. Then they were ashamed, and they tried to hide from God. (See Genesis 3:7–10.) Our disobedience drives us to hide our condition.

In a small way, I take on this shame-based thinking whenever I have to take my car in for servicing. I feel like I should know everything about cars. I hate to admit I am ignorant about some things, including cars, and I do not always fully comprehend what the technician is telling me. My fear is that the person helping me will see my needy condition or lack of expertise and take advantage of me. Some will say, "That's just a man thing," but I believe it goes far deeper than that. I believe this relates to the loss of confidence in the identity Christ gives us.

The moment Adam and Eve's teeth sunk into that fruit, sin entered the world. Humankind has been plagued by sickness, sorrow and death ever since. Sin is the root of every crime ever committed. All the deadly illnesses, like cancer and heart disease. All the atrocities committed by tyrants like Adolf Hitler and terrorists like radical Islamic extremists. All instances of fear, anger, jealousy and greed came into the world at that moment they ate the fruit.

Adam and Eve were given rule over all things "that scurry along the ground" (Genesis 1:26 NLT). They should have ruled over that serpent—after all, snakes move along the ground—but instead they let *him* rule over *them*. In an instant, they went from rulers to slaves. When they followed the unbelief he tossed at them and acted on it, a power transfer occurred. They took on Satan's position as one who would be ruled, and they gave him their position as one who had power to rule over the earth.

Satan has been using that power to destroy humanity and the earth ever since. He became the ruler, and we all became his subjects.

Humanity's unbelief empowers Satan. Our unbelief is what keeps him in power today. When we listen to his lies and act on what he says rather than on what God says, we keep his rule over us and the earth.

Think of what life was like for Adam and Eve before they accepted the false identity of sin. They walked and talked with God every day, enjoying pure communion in relationship with Him. They learned from Him and enjoyed the blessings that came from simply being in His presence.

But eating the forbidden fruit destroyed their close, one-on-one relationship with God. They were ashamed and hid from Him, who called out, "Where are you?" (Genesis 3:9). Of course, God knew where they were. He also knew they were hiding from Him—something they had never done before—instead of running to Him with open arms. They had moved away from God because of shame and fear—and fear still keeps us away from God. How different things would be if we really knew how much He loves us and desires to bless us!

God Gave You a New Identity

God had compassion on the first man and woman. He did not want them to live in shame, so this beautiful, creative, loving, benevolent God was brought to the point of taking a life to make them well. He killed an animal and made garments that would cover the shame He had never intended Adam and Eve to experience.

We do not know what kind of animal God took to make those clothes—but just suppose for a minute it was a lamb. Now, have you ever noticed that an animal without its skin or coat is hard to recognize? I was recently at a youth camp in New Zealand with about five thousand mostly Baptist teenagers. They roasted several sheep every night after the meetings.

The first night, I asked someone what kind of meat was roasting on the spit.

My host asked, "Can't you tell? It's lamb."

I replied, "If it doesn't have its skin, then its identity seems lost."

With that in mind, imagine walking into the Garden with God after the Fall. You look over and see a skinless carcass drying out in the sun, starting to decay. You ask God, "What is that?"

"That's Adam and Eve," He replies.

On the other side of the Garden, you see a couple trying to cover their nakedness under an animal skin, and you ask, "So, what is that?"

The Father replies with a smile, "Oh, that's My Lamb."

This is a parallel of how it is today. When God looks at us, He does not see our broken, rejected, useless state. He sees what He intended us to be. He sees what the Lamb sacrificed to reinstate us. We gave our identity away, so the Lamb, Jesus, came to restore that which was lost. He sacrificed to give us His identity. He clothed us in His right standing and covered us in His precious blood. His DNA was given to restore ours.

Before what Christ did for us as the second Adam, there was a need for animal sacrifices. Animals had to sacrifice their identity—their DNA, if you will—to cover ours. Even the veil in the holy of holies was made from the covering of animals, as Exodus 26:31 indicates yarn was incorporated into the making of it. Animals were sacrificed to block the view of our sin—our stolen identity caused by Satan's deception. God had such a hunger to be in the very midst of His people in the same way He had been in the Garden of Eden, and to make this possible, He had to require sacrifice. He did not want all the blood and carnage. He wanted *us*.

In the Garden of Eden, we see the perfect picture of what things were like when God spent time with humans in a very close and intimate way. It was the perfect place. God, in His benevolence, shared His authority, provision and identity with the man and woman. They enjoyed the beauty the Father gave them and the abundance of food He provided for them. He created bodies that were made to procreate and to do so with great pleasure. All creatures lived together in wonderful peace and harmony. This is a wonderful picture of who God is in His character.

The Scriptures do not give us a picture of God as a micromanager who spent all His time making sure Adam and Eve toed the line or as someone who lectured them or gave them instructions on how to manage His creation. Instead, He came into the Garden "in the cool of the day" (Genesis 3:8)—possibly early morning or evening—and just spent time with them. I imagine it was like the way a daddy and his children enjoy one another's company after he gets home from a long day at work or has been out of town for a few days. I picture Adam and Eve running to God like children, skipping joyously around Him. Maybe they wrapped their arms around His leg or even put their feet on His and danced with Him. Whatever really happened, we can be sure these visits were joy-filled and exhilarating.

I also believe these were times Adam and Eve received a greater sense of authority and permission to explore the height and depth of the power given to them by the Father. This was not the broken, skewed view of misappropriated power we have today but rather one of, "Look, guys—you can walk on water. Go ahead. Try it!"

You Can Combat the Lies

One of the ways we can combat the lies of the devil is to speak positive words of power, love and life—to tell the truth about ourselves as God sees us and to speak over others how God sees them.

A couple of years ago, when I was speaking at a conference in the Midwest, a woman came up to me and told me her adult son had become a drug addict. "My son is in such turmoil," she said. "He's living this horrible life. He's got a child, and he's not a good father. He can't keep a job. He has a terrible work ethic."

If all of that was not bad enough, she went on to tell me she had caught him stealing from her and that she'd had to kick him out of her house.

I knew she loved her son, and I did not fault her in the least for getting tough with him. I believe that was the right thing to do. I understood, too, why she wanted to tell me all the bad things her son had done, even though the list went on and on.

Finally, when I had a good understanding of the entire picture, I asked her, "What do you want for your son?"

The question seemed to startle her for just a moment.

"Well," she said, "I want him to live for God. I want him to be a good father and a good worker."

I nodded. "Okay. Why don't we do this? Every time you see him, say, 'How you doing, man of God?'"

She frowned. "But he's not."

"I know, but is that what you want him to be?"

"Of course, but . . ."

"Then every time you see him, say, 'How you doing, man of God?' And when you see him with his son, say, 'Hey, you are such a good father.'"

She looked at me as if I had lost my mind. "But he's a terrible father."

"Yes, I understand that," I said. "But whenever it's possible, I want you to point out the ways he's doing a good job. With every little improvement, just say, 'Look at that. See what a great father you are.' Also, speak out what he needs to be rather than what he's doing."

The woman's eyes narrowed as she thought about what I was saying.

I went on. "I'm not suggesting that you lie to him. We need to set boundaries and expect proper behavior. But we also need to be like Abraham, who called the things that were not as though they were.

"Your son is living under a false identity, and he needs someone to call out his true identity. As his mother, you have great influence in his life. You have great authority, and you can declare over him who he really is."

She was not convinced. "Well, I don't know if that will work," she said.

But she agreed to try it.

It was another year before I was back in her area and saw her again. She had a big smile on her face when she greeted me. "Guess what?" she said. "My son is holding down a job. He's becoming a good father. He hasn't accepted Christ yet, but I expect that to happen soon."

I was delighted, of course. "Wonderful!" I said. "Tell me what happened."

"Well, I started doing what you said to do," she said. "I began asking him what God was saying to him—what God was revealing to him in his dreams. And I kept telling him what a great father he was and what a great worker he was— and he started becoming all these things."

She continued, "It took a long time. At first, he was looking at me like I was crazy. But then he started becoming all these things."

Another year went by before I went back to the area for another conference. At that time, my new friend told me her son was still having some struggles in his life, but he was holding down a job, being a good father to his son and doing much better overall than when she had first talked to me.

"Just keep on doing what you're doing," I told her.

You Need to Know Who You Are

Now let me ask you: Do you know who you are?

I am not talking about what you have done, because that is not who you are. I am not talking about your circumstances, either, or what people say about you. I am not even talking about the scars that have been inflicted upon you or the traumas you have endured. These things may have nothing at all to do with your real identity.

The truth is, we have all had times when we have fallen down or slipped up. We have all been misunderstood or mistreated. We have all said or done things we should not have said or done. We have all fallen short of our expectations for ourselves.

But here are just a few of the things God says about us:

- "So now there is no condemnation for those who belong to Christ Jesus" (Romans 8:1 NLT).
- "So, what do you think? With God on our side like this, how can we lose?" (Romans 8:37 MESSAGE).
- "Even before he made the world, God loved us and chose us in Christ to be holy and without fault in his eyes. God decided in advance to adopt us into his own family by bringing us to himself through Jesus Christ. This is what he wanted to do, and it gave him great pleasure. So we praise God for the glorious grace he has poured out on us who belong to his dear Son. He is so rich in kindness and grace that he purchased our freedom with the blood of his Son and forgave our sins. He has showered his kindness on us, along with all wisdom and understanding" (Ephesians 1:4–8 NLT).
- "For he has rescued us from the dominion of darkness and brought us into the kingdom of the Son he loves, in whom we have redemption, the forgiveness of sins" (Colossians 1:13–14).
- "This means that anyone who belongs to Christ has become a new person. The old life is gone; a new life has begun!" (2 Corinthians 5:17 NLT).
- "For you are all children of the light and of the day; we don't belong to darkness and night" (1 Thessalonians 5:5 NLT).

- "What marvelous love the Father has extended to us! Just look at it—we're called children of God! That's who we really are. But that's also why the world doesn't recognize us or take us seriously, because it has no idea who he is or what he's up to" (1 John 3:1 MESSAGE).

All of these passages communicate what Christ came to give to us. They tell us what was reinstated to us through His death. Through Christ, we receive what was intended for us with the Tree of Life.

I believe the Tree of Knowledge of Good and Evil represents the law, or legalistic thinking. After the Fall in the Garden, we began to move toward a works-based way of life. We tried to work our way to wholeness, performing our way there. And that is where the Identity Thief wants us to stay, striving—and failing—to live according to our own righteousness.

But the Tree of Life represents Christ and His grace. Christ completed the work for us that we could never complete ourselves. We could not earn it, nor could we deserve it. If we could, that would make what Christ did a reward, rather than a gift.

No, there is no earning or deserving. There is only receiving, accepting, and living in light of what has been given. This is the truth that replaces all lies.

3

GOD USES WOUNDED WARRIORS

But he said to me, "My grace is sufficient for you, for my power is made perfect in weakness." Therefore I will boast all the more gladly about my weaknesses, so that Christ's power may rest on me.

2 Corinthians 12:9

Let me tell you about one of my heroes.[1] His name is Manny, and he is one of the boldest and most effective prayer warriors I have ever known. Manny attends a church led by a powerful pastor named Popin Perez. It was Popin and his wife, Anabel, who discipled Manny to Christ when he wandered into their church several years ago.

I would guess Manny was around twenty years old when I met him. He was born into desperate poverty in the town of Jarabacoa in the Dominican Republic, which sits in a mountain valley and is the largest city in La Vega Province. It is a beautiful setting, but underneath the beauty there is a great deal of poverty and spiritual darkness.

Manny's poverty was not the worst of his problems. Satan had a grip on his family and used his mother and siblings to try to kill him. Satan's desire to see us dead is something Manny and I have in common—although in Manny's case, Satan came much closer to succeeding. Manny told me that when he was only a toddler, his mother picked him up by both legs and slammed his body against the wall. Somehow, he survived. And that was only one of many vicious beatings he endured at her hands. Another time, one of his brothers chased him around with a knife, threatening to kill him. There were other attempts on his life, but somehow Manny always survived.

When Satan failed in his attempts to use Manny's own family to kill him, he tried polio. That, too, failed, but Manny still walks with a noticeable limp and has struggled mentally and emotionally because of the disease. He grew up not knowing what it was like to be loved and cared for. He was alternately abused and rejected, made to feel he was a worthless child.

It is really no surprise that Manny eventually turned to drugs to numb the physical and emotional pain. Tragically, that is a common problem for kids growing up in communities like this.

Manny had almost no education. Few possessions. No money. He lived in the small back room of a shop—a room that was barely big enough for him to sleep in. He was lost and alone, feeling that his life had no purpose.

But he was wrong about that. God had a purpose for him and was about to show him what it was.

By God's grace, one day Manny stumbled into Popin and Anabel's church. Before they parted ways that day, a fire was lit in his soul that only burns brighter and stronger as the years pass. On that day, he discovered his true spiritual identity. He learned that he was put on this earth to serve God and be a channel of His grace, mercy and power. Though his physical family saw nothing in him, he discovered God saw him as tremendously important to the Kingdom.

Today, Manny is someone whose face shines with joy. When he prays, things happen. God has made Manny so well known that some celebrities in Latin America come to Jarabacoa just to meet him, hang out with him and have him pray for them. Every time I go to the Dominican Republic, which has been fairly often, the first thing I ask is, "Where's Manny?"

The Devil Uses His Wiles

Now, Manny is not the only one in that church whose life was a target. Even the pastor, Popin, has seen his fair share of attempts made against him.

Let me give you a little of the background.

I gave a prophetic word to Popin that his church would be the largest in town and that he would lead the churches in that area. Many pastors were furious when they heard this word because they were jealous of Popin. He was humble, kind, very laid-back and casual in dress and style. In the Latino church culture, where pastors are treated with great respect and always are addressed by their last name with their title, such as Pastor Garcia or Pastor Hernandez, the members of his congregation simply called him Popin.

When I gave the prophetic word to Popin, I went on to say, "You will not die, you will not die, you will not die!"

Everyone looked puzzled. Popin was the picture of health, to me and to everyone else. We had no idea that not long before God spoke those words through me, Popin had been diagnosed with terminal cancer. When that happened, doctors told him he would have to have a bone marrow transplant in order to survive, and some pastors in his town began to declare he would die. Instead, he got the transplant he needed and recovered slowly.

Not long after that, a girl whose mother was a leader in the church fell from a second-floor balcony to the concrete floor below during one of the church's services. She died immediately. Popin rushed to the child and began calling her back to life, but she did not respond. He picked her up, put her in his truck and rushed her to the hospital—but it was too late.

Those who had been against Popin from the beginning said, "This will finally destroy his church." They were very nearly right. The whole congregation went into mourning. The Identity Thief was trying to destroy Popin and his church, attempting to take away their identity as God's powerful representatives of love, faith and healing in the Jarabacoa area.

But the Thief has not succeeded.

God Redeems the Wounded

Today, Popin and Anabel pastor a church full of people who once might have been considered the dregs of society. Some of the poorest and roughest people in a very poor and rough area are welcomed into the church with open arms. Young teenage boys and energetic twentysomethings fill the church. Many grew up on the streets or were involved in gangs. It is an amazing thing to see so many young men worshiping together in Latin America.

And worship they do—tough, strong young men pour out their love and adoration for God, none of them holding anything back. When I see them, I cannot help but think of these words from the apostle Paul to the church at Corinth:

> Do not be deceived: Neither the sexually immoral nor idolaters nor adulterers nor men who have sex with men nor thieves nor the greedy nor drunkards nor slanderers nor swindlers will inherit the kingdom of God. And that is what some of you were. But you were washed, you were sanctified, you were justified in the name of the Lord Jesus Christ and by the Spirit of our God.
>
> 1 Corinthians 6:9–11

Whatever those in the Corinthian church had done and wherever they had been no longer mattered, Paul said—and the same is true for all those who have come to know Christ and worship at Popin and Anabel's church. They are people who have discovered their true identity and are living it out.

I told Popin during that visit, "You know, you are sitting on top of a powder keg that is just waiting to explode. You have all these young guys who have been told their whole lives by the Identity Thief that they won't measure up, that they are trash, keeping them in a prison of low self-esteem, telling them through voices of authority and even voices in their head that they can't, that they are never going to amount to anything—but you're telling them that they can. Popin, this is powerful!"

The rest of the community had written those young men off, but Popin told them, "God is with you. God is for you. You can. You will do great things."

45

They believed him, and they are living it out. As a result, the entire community is being won to Christ. Because of faithful, courageous people like Manny, the impact of what is happening in Jarabacoa is already being felt throughout the Dominican Republic, and I believe it will soon be felt throughout all of Latin America. Satan very nearly succeeded in snuffing out the light of this vibrant congregation, but God prevailed, as He always does when we trust Him.

God Turns You into Treasure

My friends Popin and Manny are excellent examples of what happens when we refuse to listen to anything the devil says. Many people looked at Manny and saw a disabled young man who was unwanted by a family that tried to kill him. But God looked at him and saw a young lion who would rise up and cry out to God for a move of the Spirit that would leave us all breathless and speechless. Manny would shout like a prophet of old.

I can testify to this from the experience I had at a conference hosted by Popin's church recently. As my dear friend Nicole Voelkel says of what she personally witnessed in Manny during that conference:

> A more zealous man I think I have never met. Throughout the entire service, when he wasn't on his hands and knees, he was hopping from side to side on his disfigured leg across the church, calling at the top of his lungs, "Jesus! Jesus! Rain down your presence on us! Rain down your presence on us! Let it come! Let it come! Jesus, Son of God, have mercy on us! Rain down!"

Little did he know that it would literally rain on the gathering that night—during a time of year that it never rains, no less—to the point where I stopped in the middle of my teaching and said, "This isn't natural rain. This is a prophetic rain, and you'll know the Holy Spirit will rain down in this place when it suddenly stops." Sure enough, right then it stopped.

That is not the only instance when Manny demonstrated himself to be a prophet. Earlier that same afternoon, Nicole says Manny spent the afternoon in the chapel, praying and calling out, "The fire of God is coming tonight!" He had no way of knowing that earlier that same day, I had told a group of people, "Hey, guys, did you know the fire of God is falling tonight?" And then, as I have already mentioned, the Holy Spirit fell upon us through unexpected rain. Many people also experienced healing and anointing during that night of ministry.

So many of the leaders and attenders of the conference had looked at Manny on the day he shouted, "Fire will fall tonight!" and said, "Oh, look—it's crazy Manny." But he was the true prophet of the event.

Before we left to return to the States, I took off a choker I was wearing and put it around Manny's neck.

He beamed. "They have called me crazy and a fool," he said, "but now they will call me a prophet!"

I wept as I heard those words.

Manny is just one example of how Satan will take a life, call it trash and worthless, and try to destroy it. But God takes that trash and turns it into treasure. He turned Manny into a trophy for the house of God—and He will do the same for you.

Satan is full of lies and empty threats and will use whatever he can grab hold of to twist our understanding away from God's. But God will always prevail. He showed Manny and the other members of Popin's church their true identity that

Satan had stolen from them. He can and will do the same for all of us, if we only let Him.

God Uses Wounded Healers

Please do not think you have to be blameless in order for God to use you. God can and will use anyone who is available to Him. I have seen it happen again and again, so I know it is true. My church, too, was full of people who, before they met Christ, had been involved in gang violence. They had been addicted to drugs. Some had children taken away from them by the state because they were found to be unfit parents. They had been involved in every form of sexual brokenness you can think of.

But when they came to Christ, He cleansed them of all unrighteousness. After that, I saw God use them to heal the sick. I saw them prophesy and give words of wisdom and knowledge. I saw God use them to open deaf ears, to help the lame walk and to transform entire neighborhoods with the love of Christ.

We have all fallen short of God's grace. We have all been wounded one way or another. But God uses wounded healers. When we sin, we need to acknowledge that we have stepped out of our true identity, and then we need to repent. To repent means to turn around from heading in the wrong direction. In other words, just get back to where you were and who you are supposed to be. God will restore your identity every single time. You do not have to beg and plead for forgiveness. You just have to acknowledge that you got off track and then get back on it.

I know we all struggle to accept that God can use us despite our wounds and our past. Do you know how I know?

Because when I am teaching at a conference, I often ask how many people feel they are unworthy of being used by God. A few hands go up here. A few more go up over there. Pretty soon, nearly everyone in the building has raised their hand. The truth is that we all feel unqualified—but the fact that God uses us when we are not qualified is good news. Jesus gives us His qualification.

The Bible is full of examples of people who did not think they were worthy, but God used them to do great things anyway. Moses asked the Lord not to send him to talk to Pharaoh because he was "slow of speech and tongue" (Exodus 4:10). We all know what happened to Moses.

When Gideon was asked by God to liberate the Israelites from the Midianites, he replied that he was the most insignificant member of the most insignificant clan in Manasseh. (See Judges 6:15.) Yet he became a mighty general who overthrew the Midianite oppressors with an army of only three hundred soldiers.

When God appeared to Isaiah, the prophet said, "Woe to me! I am ruined! For I am a man of unclean lips and I live among a people of unclean lips, and my eyes have seen the King, the LORD Almighty" (Isaiah 6:5).

And then, of course, there is Paul, who referred to himself as the chief of sinners (see 1 Timothy 1:15)—and not without good reason. We already mentioned that he persecuted and killed the first believers of the faith before coming to a saving faith in Christ.

You are in very good company if you think you are unworthy of being used by the Lord in a mighty way. Again, the key is to remain open and honest with God, with yourself and with others regarding who you really are.

You Can Still Be Bold

Now, do not get the wrong idea and think God is pleased with false humility. That is not the case at all. If the situation demands boldness, be bold.

For example, notice what the apostle Paul said regarding this:

> I do not want to seem to be trying to frighten you with my letters. For some say, "His letters are weighty and forceful, but in person he is unimpressive and his speaking amounts to nothing." Such people should realize that what we are in our letters when we are absent, we will be in our actions when we are present.
>
> 2 Corinthians 10:9–11

Paul did not have false humility. He could be tough and assertive when the occasion called for it.

I have been called a self-promoter by people in my own movement, the Vineyard, because I am open about the healings and miracles I have seen through my ministry and because I have developed material for training that I share for people to be equipped. Of course, it grieves me when I hear something like that. I recognize the voice of the Identity Thief in these accusations.

But I am not going to stop doing what I do, because my motivation in sharing is always to talk about what the Lord has done and never what I, Robby Dawkins, have done. I share because Jesus told us, "Let your light shine before others, that they may see your good deeds and glorify your Father in heaven" (Matthew 5:16).

Another reason I share is to build faith in others by telling them about the signs and wonders that still occur and to show them how they can learn to walk in the power God always intended His people to have. One of the things I enjoy most in life is seeing what happens when other people learn to grab hold of their true identity in this way.

For example, I recently received a letter from a woman named Christa who wrote, "About two years ago my son was diagnosed with autism at the age of seven. We were living a nightmare, but would not stop chasing God for healing."

During this time, one of Christa's friends sent her a You-Tube video of my wife, Angie, and me praying for the healing of our autistic son, Canah.

Christa wrote to me:

> I copied the prayer word for word and posted it on my son's headboard, mirror, and our kitchen cabinets. I explained the prayer to my son and I prayed it every morning and every night, just as Robby and his wife did over their son. I knew the power was not in the recited prayer, but in the revelation behind the prayer. We finally had our understanding of how to attack this thing spiritually.

She went on to say, "Within a month, his symptoms started leaving one at a time. He is now at least 90 percent healed! I am doing my best to help others find freedom, too!"

Did you notice that last sentence? Christa and her family are experiencing the freedom Christ provides, and now they are doing what they can to help others find the same. Once again, it is like throwing a stone into the middle of a smooth pond full of God's grace and watching the ripples of healing move out from the center in ever-widening circles.

It reminds me of what Paul wrote to Timothy: "And the things you have heard me say in the presence of many witnesses entrust to reliable people who will also be qualified to teach others" (2 Timothy 2:2). I hate to see the period at the end of that passage. I think it should continue on to read, ". . . who will also be qualified to teach others, who will also be qualified to teach others, who will also be qualified to teach others . . . " and so on, until the whole world is full of the knowledge and power of the Lord.

The Identity Thief is working overtime to leave us feeling broken, incomplete and wounded. And we are those things, truly, until we put on the new man Christ has reinstated to us through the cross. The enemy tries to discard and reject every broken vessel, but Christ demonstrates His redemptive power by healing and using each one of us.

Be warned: We are venturing into territory here that unmasks the enemy and his plot to disqualify us. He shall not succeed. His ways are subtle and deceitful, yes, but Christ exposes the Thief's hidden agenda by tearing down the veil of darkness and inviting us to into the light. It is a light that dispels fear and strengthens you.

Will you choose that light today?

4

THE THIEF IS RELENTLESS

Be alert and of sober mind. Your enemy the devil prowls
around like a roaring lion looking for someone to devour.

1 Peter 5:8

I woke up in the middle of the night and knew immediately
that I was not in my bed.

But where was I?

At first I thought I was in a box. As I blinked into the
darkness that was brightened only by a dim light from a
small lamp beneath me, I realized my face was about eighteen
inches from the ceiling. I was floating in the air!

You can imagine my terror. What was I doing up there?
Who or what was doing this to me?

When I looked down, I saw our fearless little dog, Buddy,
sitting on the corner of my sister's bed. He looked up at me,
trembling all over.

I was sleeping in my sisters' bedroom because I had been having horrific, demonic, tormenting visitations at night and had become extremely fearful. I begged my older sisters to let me sleep on their floor that night and to leave a lamp on because I felt being with other people would stop these visitations.

At the same instant I realized I was in the air, I could make out the hooded heads of two people—or, more accurately, two beings—who were on either side of me and trying to pull my sheet over my head, moaning deeply as they did so. Somehow I knew if they succeeded, I was going to die.

Summoning every ounce of strength, I cried out, "Jesus, save me!"

As soon as the words left my mouth, the two beings disappeared and I began to float gently toward the floor.

I landed softly next to my sister's bed, looking into the face of my whimpering, trembling little dog. I pulled him next to me, desperate for his comfort and warmth.

Although my tormentors were gone, I stayed on the ground, shaking in fear, until the morning came. I did not have the strength to get up.

I told you in a previous chapter that Satan threatened to kill me before I was born but failed because my parents refused to surrender to him. As far as I know, he never appeared to them again. But that does not mean he quit trying to destroy me or steal the identity of who I was meant to be in Christ.

He tormented me through much of my childhood, in fact, before God supernaturally delivered me at the age of thirteen, not long after the time of the story I just shared with you.

Here is how it all happened.

Saved by Chewing Gum

I had gotten saved when I was seven. At the time, my parents were pastoring a small church in Atlanta, Georgia, called Baptist Chapel. It was a charismatic church where the gifts of the Spirit were always in evidence, but I suppose my parents figured you could not go wrong in the South by having the word *Baptist* in your church's name.

Early on the morning of the day I got saved, I had sneaked into my sisters' room while they were still sleeping and stolen two pieces of Wrigley's Spearmint gum. I really loved gum back then but never seemed to have any of my own. My mom had even rebuked me for pulling the black gum from underneath the pews of our hundred-year-old church and chewing it. She said that gum was old and nasty, but I found that if you chewed it enough, it became soft again and a bit of flavor was still there.

As I said, I really loved gum.

That week, three students from Georgia Tech had been staying with us and holding services every night at the church. They would give their testimonies, sing a few songs and then give an altar call. On the night of the day I stole the gum, they lit a candle in the darkened auditorium and began talking about the impact a single light can have.

I sat there in the dark, thinking, *I'm a thief. I've stolen two pieces of chewing gum. If I don't stop this pattern, I'm going to wind up in prison.*

When they gave the altar call, I ran to the front of the church.

The next night, I ran to the altar again. After the service, my mother said, "You know, son, you don't have to do that more than once."

"I know," I told her. "But I like it down here. I feel something here."

I couldn't express it at the time, but I know now that I was being drawn to the presence of God.

My mom smiled and said, "Okay. I just want to make sure you know you don't have to do this over and over again."

Those young university students did not have a powerful message to share, but they had testimonies of God's transformation. They preached the same message and told the same stories every night, but still people came to the altar again and again because the Spirit of God was moving hearts. So many of my young friends gave their lives to Christ that week, too.

Impressed by the Spirit

When I was a child, I often heard my parents speak in Japanese in church. It seemed strange to me they would use a language only they could understand. Even though they interpreted for each other so the rest of the congregation knew what was being said, I wondered, *Why speak Japanese? Why not just English?*

What was even weirder, though, was hearing others in the church speak Japanese, too, or hearing them interpret the messages my parents gave in that language.

Then, when I was nine, a speaker came to the Christian school I was attending and invited all the students to come forward to receive the baptism of the Holy Spirit. He preached from the second chapter of Acts and talked about being baptized in the Holy Spirit and speaking in tongues.

That is when I realized my parents had not been speaking Japanese all that time. They had been speaking in tongues.

The speaker said we would receive power if we received this gift of the Holy Spirit. He was very engaging and filled with passion. I thought, *Wow! I want this power. If I get it,*

I bet I'll be able to fly! When the man gave the invitation, I ran forward to the altar again. There, I found myself standing between one of the prettiest girls in school and one of the best jocks.

First, the speaker prayed for the girl, and her hands began to shake. I stood there watching in awe, expecting her to levitate at any moment. Instead, she began crying out, "Ah! Ah! I'm on fire!" Then she fell backward and hit the ground. She was shaking violently all over. I was thrilled! I was about to receive the power of all the superheroes I had ever known.

Everybody knew this girl would not fake something like that. She was very cool and sort of aloof. She was not the kind to start flopping around on the floor unless she could not help it.

I was next, but when the speaker prayed for me, nothing happened. I did not feel anything.

"Do you want to speak in tongues?" he asked.

"Yeah."

"Well, God will not withhold any good thing," he said. "I've prayed for you, and you want it, so go ahead and speak in tongues. I give you permission."

"But I don't feel anything," I protested.

"Does God lie?"

"Of course not."

"Well, then, go ahead and speak in tongues."

I began mumbling, "Brrrrrr. Brrrrr."

"You just keep doing that, and you will receive power," he said.

Then he moved on to pray for the jock. As soon as the man began to pray, this big athlete started laughing uncontrollably. Then he, too, was on the ground.

But there I stood, still not feeling a thing.

After school, I ran home and told my mom what had happened at school that day.

"That's amazing, Robby!" she said.

"But I didn't feel anything."

"Does God lie?" she asked.

"No. And why does everyone keep asking me that question? I've never accused God of lying."

My mother smiled. "So, you keep doing what you're doing—even if it's only a few minutes a day—and you're going to find power in your life."

I did as my mother said, and it was not long before I discovered what she had said was true. A few weeks later, at the playground, I asked a little girl named Tina if I could tell her about Jesus. My friends and I called her Evil Tina. She was selfish, demanding and bossy, and she tried to hog all the good stuff on the playground. If Tina was using the slide, you found something else to do because she would not share. She would even hog the teeter-totter. When I told her it took two to make the teeter-totter work, she would just hiss at me and tell me to go away.

I had tried before to talk to Tina about Jesus, and she would not listen. Her typical response was to spit on me or laugh at me. But a couple of weeks after being prayed for and practicing my tongues, I saw her on the playground and said, "Tina, I'd like to tell you about Jesus again."

To my great surprise, she said okay.

What? No spitting? No hissing at me? No head spinning backward and her spewing pea soup? (Okay, maybe I'm just being dramatic with that last one.) I was shocked that she said yes.

Being only nine, it took me about five minutes to tell Tina everything I knew about Jesus, including the fact that if she would invite Him into her heart, He would make her a new person.

She nodded and said, "I'd like to do that."

This was unbelievable. "What?" I sputtered. "I mean, you would?"

I had Tina kneel down in the sandbox, and I led her in the sinner's prayer. I honestly thought because she had been so mean to everyone that she needed to kneel in the sandbox as some sort of penitent act. I actually made her lift her little dress slightly so her knees felt the coarse sand. Poor Tina. She is probably a great evangelist somewhere right now, bringing thousands of souls into God's Kingdom every day but, confused by my example, always looking for sand before praying with others to accept Christ.

I could not wait to get home and tell my parents what had happened. When I did, my mom said, "See, that's what I was talking about when I told you that you'd have power in your life. The Holy Spirit was breathing on the words you were speaking, and that spoke to Tina."

I was blown away by that thought. God did not just speak out of the air to people? He chose to breathe on our words and actions so others would encounter Him? How generous.

Witness to God's Deliverance

Later that same year, something else happened that had a profound impact on me. I told this story in my book *Do What Jesus Did*, but I want to briefly retell it now, because it shows what can happen when we refuse to believe Satan's lies and find our true identity in Christ.

My father was a self-taught entrepreneur who had a passion for reaching people with the love of Jesus. He started several churches, a nonprofit organization and the first Christian television station in Dallas, Texas. He also dreamed of opening a home to help troubled teens—and he took his first step toward that dream by bringing home a seventeen-year-old runaway who had been living on the streets of Atlanta.

This young man, whom I'll call Pete, left home because his father beat him every day. On the streets, he had become addicted to heroin and was prostituting himself for drugs and food. Years of abuse at the hands of his father had led Pete to believe he was worthless, and he was throwing his life away.

When my dad talked to Pete about the Lord, he said he was willing to try anything that might give him a chance for a better life. So my big-hearted dad brought Pete home and put him in the extra bed in my bedroom. Outrageous? Perhaps. But it also indicates my dad's trust in Jesus. As far back as I can remember, he was always willing to take risks and step out in faith.

The first two days Pete was at our house, he went through a terrible withdrawal. He shook, sweated, cried out and vomited all over the place. I remember my mom and dad sitting there with him, my dad with his arm around the boy, praying that Jesus would deliver Pete. And on the third day, Jesus did.

I woke up early that day, just as the first rays of sunlight streamed into the room. Pete stood with his back to me, his body a silhouette against the window as he stared into our backyard.

I asked if he was okay.

When he turned around, I saw tears flowing down his face.

"Robby, it's all gone," he cried. "Jesus walked into the room this morning, and He just took it all away. The addiction, the pain, the sickness . . . my anger and shame. All of it's gone. It's just all gone."

I knew Pete was telling the truth. Everything about him seemed different. He was peaceful and calm, as if he had come safely through a raging storm—which he had. And the beautiful thing is that the change in Pete was permanent. He went on to become an integral part of Baptist Chapel and wound up going into full-time ministry as an adult.

I knew then and there, on that morning when Pete's deliverance happened, that I wanted to spend the rest of my life seeing Jesus change people just as He had changed Pete.

Stopped by Satan's Aims

Everything was going along great after that. I had surrendered myself to Jesus, experienced the infilling of the Holy Spirit and knew I wanted to spend my life serving God. I knew who I was, and my life was headed in the right direction.

Satan had other plans.

As happens to most kids, I went through a period of rebellion as I got closer to my teens. By some standards, my rebellion was pretty tame and short-lived. I was only thirteen and did not run wild, drink or use drugs. But I more or less put God on the back burner. I argued with my parents about having to spend so much time in church. I did not feel excitement or passion about God. I still remembered Jesus had come into my bedroom and taken away Pete's addiction and shame, but the thought of it did not move me to tears anymore.

A big part of the problem was that I was resentful. I did not see myself as equal to most of the kids I went to school with. My family lived and pastored in a poor part of town. After years of successful ministry, my parents were now struggling for reasons I would not find out for another several years. And even though I went to a good Christian school on a scholarship, it seemed to me most of the other kids there came from rich families. Their parents were successful doctors, attorneys and businessmen, and I felt out of place. I was also a bit resentful that my mom and dad had devoted their lives to ministry. I wanted them to give up preaching and go out and get "real jobs" so we could live in a better house, drive a nicer car and wear more fashionable clothes, as most of our clothes were from secondhand stores and thrift shops.

I also felt that our church always had the weirdest people. Most of the kids I knew went to churches that were full of "normal" people. But it seemed that to get into our church, you had to fall into the freaky, odd category. I sometimes thought when strange people showed up at one of the other churches, they were directed back to ours.

I did not want our church to grow. I wanted people to leave so my parents would get real jobs. I wanted to volunteer as an usher so I could encourage visitors not to stay. I imagined telling a visiting family, "We believe in child sacrifices here, and your little Billy seems like a great candidate." But I knew that plan would not work.

My father was always having crazy ministry ideas. When I look back, they seem quite creative, but back then I was embarrassed by most of them. For example, he took a piano moving van and converted it into a chapel on wheels. It had dim lights, carpeted floors and walls, benches on the sides and a pulpit at the front. Painted across the side, front and back, was the name Cruising Crisis Chapel. My dad even had a portable siren and yellow flashing light. We would listen to a police scanner most Friday and Saturday nights, and when a serious call came in we would jump into the Cruising Crisis Chapel, race to the scene, throw open the doors and say, "Anyone needing prayer or Jesus, come here!"

Of course, I would be praying the entire way, *Please, Lord, don't let this be one of my friends from school. I'll just die if it is.*

Most schoolday afternoons, my mother would pick me up from my private Christian school. In front of her would be a BMW, behind her a Mercedes, and there she was in the Cruising Crisis Chapel, which looked like a prop from the movie *Dumb and Dumber*. She would roll her window down and holler, "Hey, Robby, here I am—let's go! Would you like me to turn on the flashing lights or siren for your friends?"

I wanted to disappear right there.

All of these things caused me to distance myself from God. I had lost sight of who I was in Christ. The devil had stolen my spiritual identity—and that is when he began to torment me.

As I mentioned earlier, he would come to me in the middle of the night and give me horrible night terrors. I often woke up aware that an evil presence had invaded my room. I felt overwhelmed by fear and dread. I wanted to get up and run but could not. I sometimes felt demons sitting on my chest, pinning me to the bed and making it almost impossible for me to breathe or even speak. They would appear to me and say, "You will be one of us, on our side." I could not even open my mouth to call out or rebuke them in the name of Jesus. I was terrified to tell anyone because I was sure they would think I was crazy. Sometimes my bed shook and bounced. My covers were pulled off. It got so bad that I was terrified to go to bed at night. Every day, when the sun started to go down and the sky began to turn dark, I would feel fear and dread begin to pour over me.

My grades dropped dramatically because I could not concentrate on my schoolwork due to lack of sleep. I started hanging out with the dodgier kids instead of the healthier ones like before. My nighttime experiences got so bad that I asked if I could sleep in the room with my sisters. And wherever I slept, I always begged my parents to leave the light on.

The worst of those experiences happened that night I found myself floating in midair, fighting for my life against the two demons who were trying to pull my sheet over my head. They were defeated by Jesus' name that night, but I knew they would not stay away forever. Satan does not give up that easily. This kind of thing went on for months, and I thought I would never get free.

As an adult, I have met many others in ministry who told me they went through similar experiences. At many youth conferences where I have spoken, the coordinators would tell me, "Don't tell that demonic part of your story. We don't want you to scare the kids." Yet when I was permitted to tell my story, many people would come up to me afterward and say, "I've been going through that exact same thing," or, "I've experienced visitations like that in the past." Over the years, I have come to believe that such torment often comes to those who have a calling or authority on their lives to break demonic power.

All this time, I was trying to live as a decent person. I even served as the drummer for our small worship band at church. But Satan was determined to steal my identity, and I was certainly not living the victorious Christ-following life. I felt caught in a tug-of-war between God and the devil.

Rescued through a Prophetic Word

One night during this season of my torment, my family went to a service at another church in Atlanta. The Holy Spirit was really moving on the youth group there. It had gone from a handful of people in attendance to more than one thousand kids in only a month (as the story was related to us). The church grew so fast, they even knocked down their back wall and put seats in the parking lot.

When we walked in, I was shocked to discover that loud rock music filled the church. This was 1979, and at that time no one was worshiping with distorted guitar music in churches. But here they were, wailing away on their guitars and synthesizers with flashing lights, fog machines and even flash pods while young people danced in the aisles.

It was a service unlike anything I had ever seen before. These cool young people were dancing and celebrating Jesus with the uncool, weird kids—like the ones from our church—and there was no discrimination. This was stretching me in a huge way. They were shouting as they danced past, "We love You, Jesus. We'll do anything for You. We'll die for You!" I was amazed.

With a huge smile on her face, my mother asked me, "Is this the kind of music you like, Robby?"

Now, my mother hated Christian rock. To her, saying *Christian rock* was like saying *Christian atheist*. "That music was invented by the devil himself!" she would say. Yet here she was, seemingly liking it.

Well, because she loved it, I had to pretend I hated it, even though that was not true. It just could not be cool to like the same music my mom liked. So I turned to her and said, "No, I don't like it."

As the kids danced past, I grumbled, "Why are they dancing like that? Don't they know how stupid they look?"

Then a few minutes later, I wondered, *Why don't I dance like that?*

I was feeling the pull of the presence of God.

Iverna Tompkins, a prophet and preacher, was the guest speaker that night. As soon as she got up, I thought, *Why would they pick an old lady with gray hair to speak to a thousand teenagers?* But from the moment she started talking, it seemed like everything she said was an arrow aimed directly at my heart. I felt as if all the other people in the room had disappeared and she was speaking directly to me. I could not look away, even for a moment.

After Iverna finished her message, she stood still and swept the audience with her eyes, as if looking for someone.

Then she stopped and pointed in my direction. "Drummer," she said, "you're sitting over in this section, and I don't know your name, but Satan has been trying to kill you since before you were born."

My heart leapt into my throat. I knew she was talking to me. I also felt the whole room knew she was talking to me.

"As a matter of fact, Satan has been coming to you at night and tormenting you," she said. "But, Drummer, you listen to me. The Lord says to you what He said to Peter: 'Satan has tried to sift you like wheat, but I have prayed for you. And when you are turned around, I'm going to use you to strengthen your brothers and sisters all over the world.'"

At that moment, I felt as if someone had kicked me in the stomach. It was not painful, but every bit of air went out of me in an instant. *Whoosh!*

"Drummer, I want you to come down here right now because I want to pray for you," Iverna said.

I jumped out of my seat, climbed over people and ran all the way to the front.

To my surprise, I was not the only one. Five or six guys older than me were standing there, too, once I got down there, and I thought, *What are you doing here? She wasn't talking to you. She was talking to me.* Iverna pointed and nodded at me as she came off the stage. Even though I was standing in the middle of the line, she came straight to me. When she got close enough for me to hear, she said softly, "You're the one."

She said it so quietly, the others could not hear. I know now this was because she did not want to discourage any of those who had come forward. She knew they were responding to the call of the Holy Spirit in their own way. But I also know God meant that word for me, because the word she gave was so specific.

Iverna put her hands on my shoulders and prayed a simple prayer. Her prayer was not dramatic or powerful. I do not even remember the exact words she used. But I knew she had authority, and I had been set free.

I left the service that night on fire for God. I went from sitting in the back row of church to the front row. My parents had always insisted that my sisters and I be in church every time the doors were open. In our case, that was several times a week, and sometimes I had resented that. Not anymore. Instead, I hated the nights when we did *not* have church— because I could not get enough.

Iverna Tompkins's prophetic word to me had also crystallized God's purpose for my life. God was definitely calling me into ministry, to "strengthen my brothers all over the world," as the prophetic word she shared had testified. I knew I had an identity, a sense of great purpose.

This confirmed what had happened a few months before, too, when I was in the midst of my rebellion and resentment but the Holy Spirit had spoken to me during a service at my church. During the worship time, my dad had begun giving a message in tongues. This was not unusual by any means, but this message went on for a couple of minutes or more—longer than usual.

As I sat with my head bowed as my dad gave the message that day, I asked the strangest question. *Lord*, I prayed silently, *are You calling me into the ministry?*

Almost as soon as that prayer went up, my dad stopped speaking and my mother gave the interpretation. In a strong, clear voice, she said, "The Lord wants you to know the answer is yes!"

I nearly passed out.

My dad looked at my mother as if she must have something more to say. Surely, the message he had given in tongues that had gone on so long would not be interpreted in a mere fifteen seconds. But my mother said nothing more, and I knew God was speaking directly to me.

Instructed by the Example of Jesus

Still, even at the age of thirteen, I knew Satan was not done with me. I knew this because he did not even let up on Jesus after trying to tempt Him in the wilderness. Luke 4:13 says, "When the devil had finished all this tempting, he left him [Jesus] until an opportune time."

I had a greater sense of God's power and presence after that youth service, sure, and I knew I could rely on God to defeat the devil—worship became a big weapon for me in that regard—but I knew Satan was not done. He never gives up. He is like one of those characters in a horror movie. You think he has been defeated, but he suddenly comes roaring back to life in the last few minutes.

Still, something powerful happens for us when we withstand him. And we can learn how to do this by looking to that example of Jesus in the wilderness, knowing Satan uses the same sort of tricks on us today.

In Luke 4, we see Jesus being challenged in the central area of His identity. To set the stage, remember that Satan appeared to Jesus after Jesus' baptism and quoted Scripture in an attempt to get Jesus to disbelieve His identity and distrust His heavenly Father. It was the same strategy Satan used in the Garden of Eden, if you will remember. And Satan knew that if he succeeded, Jesus would no longer be the perfect Lamb who was to be sacrificed for the sins of the world.

Let us take a look at what happens.

Questioning the Word of God

First we see in the book of John that John the Baptist—the greatest of all the prophets, according to Jesus (see Matthew 11:11)—shouted, "Look, the Lamb of God, who takes away the sins of the world!" (John 1:29, 36). Then, in the third chapter of Luke, we read that as Jesus was being baptized, the Holy Spirit descended on Jesus in the form of a dove and that the Father spoke from heaven, saying to Jesus, "You are my Son, whom I love" (Luke 3:22).

So we see the Holy Spirit, the heavenly Father and the greatest of all the prophets declaring who Jesus is. Then we are given details about Jesus' genealogy that traces His family history all the way back to Adam (see Luke 3:23–38), which is the fourth powerful witness to the divinity of Christ, as it confirms the prophecies of His family line.

Still, Satan challenges Christ's identity. He does this first by appealing to Jesus' hunger, knowing Jesus has not eaten anything for forty days: "The devil said to him, 'If you are the Son of God, tell this stone to become bread'" (Luke 4:3). Notice the enemy was challenging Jesus' identity by saying, "If you are the Son of God." Remember, the Father knew who Jesus was, the Holy Spirit knew who Jesus was, and the greatest of all the prophets, John the Baptist, knew who Jesus was. Satan also knew, but he wanted to see if Jesus knew His own identity. If Jesus demonstrated the slightest bit of uncertainty, then Satan would pounce upon that opening to achieve victory and destroy God's plan of redemption for mankind.

Satan challenged the word that the Father, the Holy Spirit, John the Baptist and Jesus' genealogy declared over Him. Even so, Jesus used the Word of God to refute the devil's claims. He answered the devil's challenge by saying, "It is written: 'Man shall not live on bread alone'" (Luke 4:4).

Jesus quotes Logos—the Word of God—because that is who Jesus is. As my mother used to always teach, "His eternal name isn't Jesus. His eternal name is written on His thigh: *the Word of God.*" Here, Jesus is establishing His identity by letting Satan know He knows who He is and that He is fully authorized as the Word of God. He references Scripture as the authority, therefore referencing Himself as the authority.

Satan was hoping to take advantage of Jesus in His lesser condition—in other words, in His human form. He did not see Jesus in the awe-inspiring way He is described in the first chapter of Revelation or the tenth chapter of Daniel: His eyes blazing like fire, His hair white as snow, His garments glowing white and His voice like thunder. Instead, starving in His human condition, Jesus looked like a mere mortal.

Satan must have thought, *Surely, something has gone wrong. Here is my chance to bring Him down.* He said, in essence, to the Lord, "Just look at You in this pitiful human form. Your clothes are dirty, Your stomach aches from hunger and, after forty days in the wilderness, You could use a bath about now. Aren't You suppose to be the Bread of Life? And speaking of bread, why don't You prove who You are by turning these stones into bread?"

Jesus never fell for this "prove it" argument. Even when the same argument was hurled at Him later at His trial and crucifixion, He never responded to the challenge to prove His divinity. To do so would be to acknowledge Satan's authority and power. Instead, Jesus proved His power and identity by not reacting.

Challenging the Worship of God

When his first effort did not work, Satan went after Jesus' worship. He appealed to Christ's knowledge that he, Satan, is the rightful ruler of this world—and that he won that right in the Garden of Eden:

> The devil led him up to a high place and showed him in an instant all the kingdoms of the world. And he said to him, "I will give you all their authority and splendor; it has been given to me, and I can give it to anyone I want to. If you worship me, it will all be yours."
>
> Luke 4:5–7

Satan is saying, "Jesus, let's do this the easy way rather than the hard way. Your Father is trying to make You suffer unnecessarily. Just bow down to me, and I'll give the world back to You." But Jesus answered, "It is written: 'Worship the Lord your God and serve him only'" (Luke 4:8).

It is worth noting Jesus did not dispute Satan's claim that all the kingdoms of the world belonged to him. He did not dispute it because it was—and is—true. Remember, Adam and Eve handed the kingdom of this world over to Satan in the Garden of Eden.

Yet Jesus quotes the Word of God again. He stands again on His authority.

Twisting the Word of God

With Jesus quoting Scripture yet again, Satan tried another tactic: using God's Word, too, but twisting it for the purpose of his selfish ambition and agenda:

> The devil led him to Jerusalem and had him stand on the highest point of the temple. "If you are the Son of God," he said, "throw yourself down from here. For it is written: 'He will command his angels concerning you to guard you carefully; they will lift you up in their hands, so that you will not strike your foot against a stone.'"
>
> Jesus answered, "It is said: 'Do not put the Lord your God to the test.'"
>
> Luke 4:9–12

We learn from this that if Satan cannot get to you with one attempt, he will try another. Often he attacks when we think we are at our strongest. It is just at that moment, when we are feeling confident about ourselves, that he catches us off guard.

And yet Jesus does not react to the taunts of the Identity Thief. Rather, we see Him quote the Word of God—His true identity—to extinguish the Thief's plot to derail God's purpose.

Because the Identity Thief is jealous of us for bearing the image of God, he will seek to derail us, too. He will always seek to distract us from our greater purpose by appealing to our desires in the moment. When that happens, we need to respond the same way Jesus did in the desert. We need to keep our eyes on the work the Lord is seeking to accomplish through us. God's provision is always there for those who "seek first his kingdom" (Matthew 6:33).

Carried by the Grace of God

Satan worked hard to torment me with fear and to deplete my sense of value through lies. I believe he knew God had a greater purpose for me—one of equipping the Body of Christ to defeat the enemy's kingdom—and that is why he tried to kill me at birth. I also believe he pounced on me when he saw my struggle with the kind of life my parents had chosen to live in ministry.

How, then, can we defeat the enemy of this world? Only with God's help and only by remaining constantly vigilant. Do not trust what you feel, but rather trust what God says about you. Hold to God's declaration over you. Understand that "the one who is in you is greater than the one who is in the world" (1 John 4:4). In other words, trust what the Word of God says about you rather than what the Identity Thief says about you or what you might be feeling in the moment.

I always reflect on the following passages to do this. James 4:7–8 says, "Submit yourselves, then, to God. Resist the devil, and he will flee from you. Come near to God and he will come near to you." The battle is not ours to fight. It belongs to the Lord. And He has already won it! But there is a need to continue to walk out that victory Christ has won.

In the seventh chapter of Romans, Paul talks about his struggles to do what is right:

Although I want to do good, evil is right there with me. For in my inner being I delight in God's law; but I see another law at work in me, waging war against the law of my mind and making me a prisoner of the law of sin at work within me. What a wretched man I am! Who will rescue me from this body that is subject to death? *Thanks be to God, who delivers me through Jesus Christ our Lord!*

Romans 7:21–25, emphasis added

Take another look at the last sentence in that passage. Paul is saying he has already been delivered from this inner turmoil through what Christ has already done for him.

The same is true of you and me. Through faith in Christ, we have been delivered from everything Satan tries to do to us. When he attacks, we must remember our true identity that Christ reinstated to us. We need to stay as close to Him as possible and take any contrary thought Satan throws at us captive by viewing it in the light of what Jesus says about us.

When Paul says that sin was "waging war against the law of [his] mind and making [him] a prisoner" (verse 23), we learn that the battlefield is in the mind and will. The only way to win the battle is to recognize that Jesus has already broken the chains of our false, Satan-imposed identity. Jesus has released us from the chains that kept us bound and has showed us how to think in a different way that renews our minds. He has shown us a new and living way.

5

STAY PLUGGED IN

"I am the Vine, you are the branches. When you're joined with me and I with you, the relation intimate and organic, the harvest is sure to be abundant. Separated, you can't produce a thing."

John 15:5 MESSAGE

Carol and her husband, John, were active members in a church that taught that the age of miracles was over. Anybody who believed in signs and wonders was suspect. In fact, Carol served as an elder and saw one of her primary duties to be that of protecting the congregation from charismatic influences. People who seemed to believe in such things were told they were not welcome there.

Then one day, the couple's three-year-old son, Sean, wandered away from their home. Carol had just noticed he was no longer in the yard when she heard screams coming from a garden across the road. Carol called out for her husband, and they ran as fast as they could in the direction of the screams.

There Sean was, running down the street, his arms flailing at a cloud of honeybees swarming around him. The toddler had wandered into a neighbor's set of hives and had been stung numerous times.

John and Carol picked him up, pulled off his shirt, brushed the bees from his body and carried him home. By the time they reached the safety of their house, angry red welts had appeared all over his body.

Carol remembers John did something he had never done before. He laid his hands on their young son and prayed that Jesus would heal him.

"John prayed desperately," Carol says. "And something extraordinary happened. The fifty or so welts that covered his body disappeared until finally there wasn't a mark left on him and he slept peacefully. Not surprisingly, we were thrilled. God had spared our son."

After that, as often happens when God supernaturally answers our prayers, doubts began to creep in. Maybe the bee stings had not been as bad as they had first thought. Or perhaps Sean was naturally immune to bee venom. Whatever it was, John and Carol pretty much forgot about it and went back to fighting those who taught that the supernatural gifts of the Spirit are available for Christians today.

It was not until thirteen years later that Carol had a dream that changed everything. In her dream, she was standing on a soapbox, doing what she describes to have been her "usual anti-charismatic teaching." But when she woke up, she found herself speaking in tongues.

"The next moment I could hardly breathe under the weight of conviction of sin," she says.

Over the next month, she went back to more than thirty people from her church, asking them to forgive her for how she had treated them. Soon, many of these people joined together in worship, prayer and seeking God, and God met them in a mighty way.

The people I just told you about are Carol and John Wimber, who became the leaders of Vineyard International, an international fellowship of churches that includes some fifteen hundred congregations. Among other things, the Vineyard has been noted for its belief in healing, prophecy and power evangelism, in which the preaching of the Gospel is accompanied by signs and wonders. I have been a part of the Vineyard since 1996, after coming in contact with the movement through the Toronto Blessing, which I will share more about later on. There have been many twists and turns in this movement, and I believe Satan has worked very hard to steal the Vineyard's true identity.

For years, the Wimbers turned their backs on the power God makes available to His children. As a result, they did not receive the miracles and blessings God wanted to give them. Please do not let that happen to you or anyone else.

The Bible says, "You do not have because you do not ask God" (James 4:2). The apostle Paul also offers harsh words to those who have a form of godliness but deny its power (see 2 Timothy 3:5). There is only one thing we need to do to appropriate the power that God has made available to us, and that is to live close to Jesus Christ and be available for God to use us whenever we see an opportunity.

In my first book, *Do What Jesus Did*, I explain that Jesus did not come to earth as a human being just to show us what He could do as the Son of God. According to the second chapter of Philippians, He set aside His "God powers" and came as a normal human being, empowered by the Holy Spirit. Jesus came to restore the lost dominion that was given away by Adam and Eve in the Garden of Eden. In other words, He did not come to show us what *He* could do, but rather to show us what *we* can do as human beings operating in our restored identity.

Do You Know the Power in You?

I read a story about a homeless woman in New York City who inherited something like $50 million. For nearly three years, the authorities were trying to track her down and tell her she was rich. Meanwhile, she was sleeping in alleys, eating food she had fished out of Dumpsters and begging for spare change from strangers. She could have been eating in the finest restaurants in town and sleeping in comfort in the best hotels, but she did not know what she had or who she was.

It is tragic to think so many Christians are struggling in a similar way when they do not need to, either. They do it because they do not have a proper understanding of what it means to be an heir of God. We are the richest people in the world! We cannot go back and start digging in trash cans again. We have to remember that the only way this world will see God is to see Him in us.

God's plan of hope and salvation for the world is Christ in you. If you have been praying for revival or a mighty move of God in your city, your area or even your family, that revival or move of God is reading these words right now. It is Christ in you!

Putting this another way, do you ever wonder how many times God protects you or blesses you in some way and you are not even aware of it? It happens every day. Satan does everything he can to cause us trouble and harm, but he cannot get through the protection God has put around us.

For example, imagine you are on your way to work and you seem to hit every red light. Or maybe you decide to take an alternate route for some reason. Could God be slowing you down or changing your path to prevent you from getting involved in a serious crash? Maybe you are being hindered to be a God encounter for someone else.

I believe when we stay in sync with Jesus, our steps are guided by the Holy Spirit, even though we may not always realize it. It is as if God and the devil are playing a game of chess, and the devil simply cannot win.

If you are a sports fan at all, you know the Harlem Globetrotters always play an opponent called the Washington Generals. These two basketball teams have played thousands of games against each other, and the Globetrotters always win. Satan is just like the Washington Generals. He never wins, but he will not give up. He is a hapless, defeated foe. However, he can still pack a punch when we are not vigilant.

There is no limit to the great things we will accomplish if we stay plugged in to our Power Source and operate in our true identity, as Jesus taught us to do. Because we are God's children, the things we do and the words we speak have a special power attached to them. Hearts will be touched for God and lives changed in a way we cannot even begin to imagine. This is part of our spiritual identity.

Has the Power Used You?

Sometimes God protects us and uses us in a big way at the same time. I know I have experienced that. The first time it happened, it was not so long after that word of knowledge Iverna Tompkins spoke to me.

As you can imagine, that word of knowledge changed everything. I got out my dusty Bible and started reading it. Power and light seemed to jump off every page in a way I had not experienced in a long time.

I told my dad, "We've got to start one of those bands at our church."

My dad, always one to step out in faith, thought it was a great idea. If it was a way to reach more people for Jesus, he was all for it.

We already had a small band that played at church services, but it was a long, long way from being a rock band. We were going to have to undergo a major transformation.

Another obstacle that stood in our way was the fact that I was not a very good drummer. I was adequate, but I was only thirteen and had not been playing that long. The other guys in the band were older, and I think they saw me as their temporary drummer until someone with more ability came along.

Funny thing about that, though. After hearing God speak to me through Iverna Tompkins, I was a much better drummer.

"What happened to you?" the other guys asked. "How did you learn to play like that?"

I could not explain it, but it was obvious to me, too. I felt more comfortable behind the drums. Certainly part of that was due to my newfound confidence, but I think there was something supernatural behind it as well. God was increasing my talent because He saw how much I wanted to use it for His glory. I honestly felt that when Iverna called me out by saying, "Drummer . . . ," it was like the Lord was calling me out in my identity. I actually became a better drummer after that. I am not saying I was drumming like Keith Moon or John Bonham, but neither was I an embarrassment back there.

To kick our band up a notch, we took over an old, run-down garage behind the church and turned it into a band shell. We installed our own light system by drilling holes in paint cans and putting light receptacles in them. We could not afford colored gels to put on the lights, so we bought clear, plastic notebook covers—reds, blues and greens—and taped them over the lights. Those notebook covers always melted about three-quarters of the way through a performance.

Our guitar player and songwriter, Bruce, and I also used gunpowder to make our own flash pods, because we could not afford the real thing. We always had to wait until the last song to set off those flash pods because they stung our eyes and irritated our lead singer's throat, making it impossible for us to go on. Between those melting notebook covers, the homemade wiring and the gunpowder, I am surprised we did not burn that garage down! I suppose that was another way God looked out for us.

Our band, which was called Power, played concerts in that converted garage for three years every Saturday night. We did not bring in great crowds. Most of the time, 25 or 30 people came to hear us. We were really pumped up when we had 50 people in the audience. One time, we played to an overflow crowd of 75.

Still, despite the fact that we were not exactly bringing in enough people to fill Atlanta's Fulton County Stadium, a few people were being saved, and that was all we really cared about. With my dad working the soundboard, my mother on the lights and sometimes keyboards, and my sisters, Debbie and Ella, as backup singers, Power was truly a Dawkins family affair.

Now, we certainly were not the best band in the world. In fact, we may have been one of the worst. But we were loud and enthusiastic, and that counts for an awful lot when it comes to rock music. Also, improvement came with time, and we gained some celebrity about town.

The high point came when we were invited to give a Saturday evening concert on the front lawn of a Methodist church in the area.

We did not have a portable drum stage, but my dad had found some old scaffolding in the area, and he had an idea.

"Hey, let's use the scaffolding to make a drum stage," he suggested.

Sure. Why not? It seemed like a great place to set up my drum kit, even though I would be situated about six feet above the rest of the band. Once again, God had provided.

We hoisted the drums onto the scaffolding, and it looked kind of weird, but it gave me a good view of our biggest-ever audience—probably around two hundred people. I was thrilled, not because we were going to get to play in front of so many people, but because it presented us with a wonderful opportunity to share Jesus, and I was not about to waste it.

Everything went fine, at first. We would play a few songs, give a brief Bible message, then play a few more songs and so on. People seemed to be enthusiastic, smiling and clapping along to the music.

About halfway into the event, though, when I was preaching from my scaffold about how Jesus went to the cross on our behalf, a man came around the side of the building behind me, waving his arms and screaming angrily. I could not understand everything he said, but I did hear him say, "Stop this right now!" I also heard a lot of words I cannot repeat and something about killing somebody.

The guy was extremely agitated, and he was making threats. But I figured he was mentally ill and essentially harmless and that the best thing we could do was ignore him. After all, there were a lot of crazy people in the area. I also knew Satan had sent the man to interrupt me because my words were making an impact for Christ.

I responded by getting closer to the mic and talking louder so people could hear me over the man's shouting. My training had always been that if you are addressing a crowd and a distraction arises, never give up the mic or allow someone else to take over because you will lose the crowd.

Sure enough, as I continued speaking, the guy quit yelling. But then my platform began to shake. To my shock, the guy had climbed up on the scaffold and was now standing behind me.

I was annoyed but not scared. I kept preaching, because I could see the crowd was fully attentive. People seemed to be hanging on every word, and I began to think, *I'm only fifteen years old, but I must be doing a good job, because everyone is being so quiet and focused.*

I looked into the audience and saw my dad waving his arms. I thought, *Wow! This must be powerful preaching, because even my dad is getting touched by it.*

My mother was sitting close, and she, too, was looking up at me and waving. Were those tears rolling down her cheeks? *I've got to remember this passage,* I thought. *This must be powerful stuff to get them to react like that.* After all, they were both very powerful and gifted speakers.

The guy reached out and tapped me on the back of the head several times. I completely ignored him and kept going.

Despite his antics, I could see all eyes were still on me, and people seemed to be reacting with deep emotion to every word I said. I looked down at our bass player and saw his gaze was fixed on me, his jaw hanging open.

The guy tapped me on the head again, and I ignored it again. At that point, he stopped shouting, became quiet and stood there for several minutes. I guess he had decided he could not rattle me. Then he climbed back down to the ground. *It's about time*, I thought.

I paused a moment in my preaching, intending to let a thought I had just shared sink in for people, and the pastor of the church stepped in front of the band and grabbed our lead singer's mic.

"I'm sorry if anybody was offended," he shouted in a shaky voice. "God bless you. The concert is over. Go on home now."

What is he doing? I thought. *Why is he interrupting me before I even get to the "come to Jesus" part?*

Whatever his reason might have been, it was clear the concert was over, and there was nothing I could do but lay down my drumsticks and sit there, trying to figure out what had just happened.

Our bass player, Dexter, came over and quickly climbed halfway up the scaffolding.

"Dude! That was awesome," he said.

"I know," I agreed. "I'll have to remember to use this passage of Scripture again. It was really great stuff. Did you see how the crowd was hanging on every word?"

"Passage of Scripture?" he said. "I'm not talking about that. I'm talking about the guy holding the gun to your head."

"G-g-gun?"

My legs suddenly went weak, and my stomach lurched as if I were riding the world's most terrifying carnival ride. I had not seen any gun. And I certainly would not have ignored the guy if I had known he was tapping the back of my head with a loaded pistol.

"Yeah!" Dexter continued. "The guy was holding a gun to your head, and you just kept on talking. That was crazy!"

I found out later the man who had threatened to blow my head off walked over to the pastor after the concert and said, "I need what that boy has."

When the pastor started to apologize for upsetting him so much, the fellow interrupted him.

"You don't understand," he said. "I have to have what that boy has. Even when I held a gun to his head, he believed so much in what he was talking about that he was fearless and just kept speaking. I need that in my life."

The man wound up praying with the pastor to receive Christ. Last I heard, he was still part of that church.

After the event, I tried not to let anyone know that my knees were banging together as we loaded our gear into the Cruising Crisis Chapel. They were still shaking as we all squeezed in for the drive back to our part of town.

As we made our way through the streets, the Lord spoke to me, saying, *That's how I want you to live.*

I thought, *Stupid, naïve, ignorant? Yeah. I can do that.*

He continued, *I don't want you to ever live with the fear that you might be taken out before your time. I don't want you to worry that you will leave this earth one day too soon or stay one day too late. I want you to live as if every day is in My hands.*

It is absolutely true. The Lord will use you if you live as if each day is in His hands. As the psalmist says, "Your eyes saw my unformed body; all the days ordained for me were written in your book before one of them came to be" (Psalm 139:16).

Once again, the lesson from all of this is that God can use you in a mighty way, even when you do not really know what is going on. God is working to establish our identity even when we are trying to understand that identity. That day on the church lawn, God accomplished His work through me, even though I was unaware of it.

Are You in Sync with the Power?

Have you ever noticed that when a man and woman are married to each other for a long time, they start to look like each other? That's pretty good news for most of the men I know. Not so great for the ladies. (Just kidding, guys!)

Daniel Goleman, writing in the *New York Times*, says:

> Science is lending support to the old belief that married couples eventually begin to look alike.
>
> Couples who originally bore no particular resemblance to each other when first married had, after 25 years of marriage, come to resemble each other, although the resemblance may be subtle, according to a new research report.
>
> Moreover, the more marital happiness a couple reported, the greater their increase in facial resemblance.
>
> The increase in facial similarity results from decades of shared emotions, according to Robert Zajonc, a psychologist at the University of Michigan, who did the research.[1]

Do you want to look like Jesus? Spend time with Him!

A bit earlier, we talked about the wonderful relationship Adam and Eve enjoyed with God before they ate the forbidden fruit. Every day, they had the privilege of walking with Him in the Garden of Eden, drinking from the cup of His love and wisdom.

The Bible refers to Jesus as "the last Adam." First Co-rinthians 15 says, "For as in Adam all die, so in Christ all will be made alive" (verse 22). A little further down in the chapter, Paul says:

> So it is written: "The first man Adam became a living being"; the last Adam, a life-giving spirit. The spiritual did not come first, but the natural, and after that the spiritual. The first man was of the dust of the earth; the second man is of heaven. As was the earthly man, so are those who are of the earth; and as is the heavenly man, so also are those who are of heaven. And just as we have borne the image of the earthly man, so shall we bear the image of the heavenly man.
>
> 1 Corinthians 15:45–49

I believe we are to bear Christ's image not only when we get to heaven, but here and now on earth. We are to be like Him, doing the things He did and saying the things He said. Jesus said, "Very truly I tell you, whoever believes in me will do the works I have been doing, and they will do even greater things than these, because I am going to the Father" (John 14:12). When we spend time with God, our lives line up with His will and we are able to do the same miracles Jesus did.

The Holy Spirit has given us the power to do as Jesus did. We just have to activate it. Unfortunately, we often miss this step. It is just like the old story of an unsatisfied customer who took a chainsaw back to the hardware store where he had bought it.

The sales clerk asked, "What seems to be the matter with it?"

"It just doesn't work," the disgruntled customer said. "It takes me forever to saw through the smallest piece of lumber."

"Hmm. Let me take a look," said the clerk. He pulled the cord, and the chainsaw roared to life.

The customer jumped back in surprise and fear. "What on earth is that noise?" he shouted.

You see, the man had the power—it was right there in his hands—but he did not know how to use it.

As the last Adam, Christ understood the importance of spending time with His heavenly Father. Everywhere Jesus went during His earthly ministry, He was besieged by crowds of people. Many were desperate for a healing touch. Others wanted to hear the wisdom that came from His lips. Still others just wanted to get a look at this man who was being hailed by some as the Messiah. Remember the paralytic's friends? They were the ones described in Mark 2:1–12 who cut a hole in the roof of the house where the Lord was staying and lowered their pal into the room on a mat because it was the only way they could get close to Him. That gives us a pretty good idea of the crowds Jesus attracted.

Yet despite the multitudes of people who crowded around Him, Jesus often looked for an opportunity to get away to a quiet place so He could spend one-on-one time with His Father. It seems clear His disciples often saw Jesus in prayer because they asked Him, "Lord, teach us to pray" (Luke 11:1). Because Jesus spent so much time with His Father, He could say, "I'm telling you this straight. The Son can't independently do a thing, only what he sees the Father doing. What the Father does, the Son does. The Father loves the Son and includes him in everything he is doing" (John 5:19–20 MESSAGE). Again, if you remain connected to Jesus and use the authority He gave you, you will be able to do the things Jesus did.

Will You Step Out in Power?

Now, understand that when I see someone who needs healing, I do not stop and ask, "Father, do You want me to pray for him?" Rather, the very fact that I recognize someone's need for healing shows I have the Father's heart for them, and I know He always wants to heal. My task is to participate with God in what He is doing to meet the need in someone's life. When I am in sync with God, I know what to do. Because I spend time with Jesus, I begin to take on His desires, and when I act on those desires to pray for people, they are often healed on the spot.

It is true, too, that I do not always pray for every sick or injured person I see. My wife does not want me to minister to people when we are on a date night, for example. That is cool by me, because I need to be focused on her those nights, letting God use me to show her how much value she has as my wife and as His daughter.

God can and will stir your heart with great compassion for people who desperately need to hear a word from Him, and He will prompt you regarding what to say to them. You will see people come into the Kingdom as you begin to step into doing signs and wonders. He will back you up. When you are in sync with God and God gives you a nudge or a specific directive to pray for someone, I see it as a perk.

I have had people tell me they are waiting on God to move. But the truth is that He is waiting on *us* to move. Just like the homeless woman who did not know she was a millionaire, we have to reclaim our true identity.

Jesus said if we are ashamed of Him, then He will be ashamed of us when He comes back to the earth with His angels (see Mark 8:38). When I hear believers pray as if they are trying to operate in some sort of stealth mode, I wonder if they are battling that shame. We cannot give in to the fear that we will look foolish if we pray for someone and they do not get healed. That type of stealth thinking actually works against the signs-and-wonders process.

I believe the Church has heard too many sermons about self-improvement and self-betterment. I believe a steady diet of these topics leads to self-preservation. Self-preservation is the death of faith for the Church. After all, Jesus said, "For whoever wants to save their life will lose it, but whoever loses their life for me will find it" (Matthew 16:25).

It is almost like we see someone who needs healing and we whisper, "Pssssst. I see that you need prayer. But I know how embarrassing it can be to be prayed for in public. So come over here behind this tree or behind this wall so no one can see us, and I'll pray for you. That way I won't embarrass you."

People do not want anyone to see them praying for healing because they are afraid nothing will happen. When someone needs prayer, they say, "I'll keep you in my prayers," but they don't stop and say, "Let me pray for you right now." They eliminate the risks real faith requires.

Faith, though, is spelled R-I-S-K. God wants us to walk in our original identity and for us to act boldly. Why? Because Jesus acted boldly. If we stay plugged in to the Power Source, then we will be willing to engage in risky living—in faith living—and we will see miracles happen as a result. We must be willing to risk being embarrassed for the sake of God's Kingdom.

Here is the truth: We are meant to be bold, courageous and strong as we do the works of Jesus. We are not supposed to blend in. We are supposed to stand out. We are supposed to be lights in the world—but that can only happen if we are willing to stay plugged in and flip on the switch.

Have You Experienced Power Like This?

My son Judah was in a burger restaurant not long ago when he encountered another boy about his age with a broken leg. The boy's leg was wrapped in a cast from toe to knee, and he was using crutches.

"What happened?" Judah asked.

"I broke my leg a few days ago," the boy said.

"Does it hurt if you put pressure on it?"

"Yes, it does."

"Well," Judah said, "if you let me pray for you right now, Jesus will completely heal your leg. He wants to show you how much He loves you and wants a relationship with you. So, can I pray for you?"

The other boy shrugged his shoulders. "Okay, I guess."

Judah asked the boy to put a little weight on his leg to heighten the pain so they could measure the progress of healing after the prayer. The boy said the pain was about a twelve on a scale of one to ten.

"Hey, everybody," Judah shouted, getting the attention of everyone in the restaurant. "You wanna see someone get healed? Come over here. A miracle is about to take place!"

About ten other kids came to see what was going on. One of them was openly skeptical.

"I'm an atheist," the skeptical one said. "I don't believe in this stuff."

"Oh, then you need to get real close," Judah said.

What was Judah doing? He was stepping out in faith. He was building an atmosphere of expectancy and faith by increasing the environment of risk. When he said to the kid with the broken leg, "God is going to heal you right now so you know He loves you and wants a relationship with you,"

Judah was not giving a prophetic word but rather increasing risk. Remember, faith is spelled R-I-S-K.

One thing he was *not* doing, though, was putting God to the test. Because Judah knows our heavenly Father wants to heal, he had complete confidence God would respond in compassion and mercy.

Self-preservation says, "Sneak away and pray for someone out of plain sight if you're not sure God will respond." But risk says, "Put more on the line. Get more public with it." If you feel a little scared or nervous, that is exactly when you need to picture risk, or faith, like a valve and start turning it up. Whispering for someone to join you in a hidden place only turns the valve of risk down.

That day, Judah prayed for the boy with the broken leg. After the first prayer, the boy's pain level went from a twelve down to a two. Then Judah prayed a second time and the pain level dropped to zero. That young man began walking around without crutches, putting his full weight on the leg and having no pain whatsoever.

Judah turned and looked at the group that had gathered to watch.

"Jesus healing this kid's leg was Him inviting you all to have a relationship with Him," he said. "Now, how would you like to respond to Jesus' invitation to you?"

And all who saw, including that young atheist, were impacted for God.

Do You Believe in Healing Power?

Not long ago, a woman came to me and told me her son was a cessationist—in other words, he believed the age of miracles was over.

"He doesn't believe this is real," she said. "Would you take him out on the streets with you?"

Now, cessationists believe signs and wonders were used to establish the Church in the first century but have since been done away with. They base this partially on a misreading of 1 Corinthians 13, where Paul says:

> Love never fails. But where there are prophecies, they will cease; where there are tongues, they will be stilled; where there is knowledge, it will pass away. For we know in part and we prophesy in part, but when completeness comes, what is in part disappears.
>
> verses 8–10

Nevertheless, the woman's son was willing to go with me as I ministered to people on the streets of the city. He was with me as I gave specific words of knowledge to people, and he saw some healings take place.

We had with us several members of a professional film crew who were making a documentary on the identity message that I teach. Tiffany, one of the camera operators and creators of the movie, noticed a deaf man handing out sign language alphabet cards for donations. I approached him and began to talk to him in sign language, something I learned as a young man in my father's church.

Although my sign language was a bit rusty, the man understood me when I asked him if he had any physical needs I could pray about. He replied that he was in agony from pain in his feet.

I prayed for him two or three times before a smile appeared on his face and he told me the pain was gone.

I then asked the young man with me to pray for the man's hearing to be restored. Remember, this young man did not believe healing still happens in our time. With some reluctance, he put his hands over the man's ears and began to pray.

He prayed once. Nothing.

Twice, and again nothing.

The third time, the deaf man looked startled. Something was definitely happening.

My young friend prayed again, and one of the deaf man's ears opened. A huge smile spread across his face as he realized he was hearing for the first time ever.

He began to turn his head at every sound. "What was that?" he kept asking. The man could hear.

I should pause here and say that healing does not always come the first time you pray. But if you keep at it, it will come, even if it takes weeks, months or years—though in my own experience this is rare. In my encounter with the deaf man, just as with Judah and the boy with the broken leg, more than one prayer was necessary. (By the way, whenever I pray for someone, I always ask them to be honest with me and not nice to me. I do not want anyone to tell me they have been healed if it has not really happened.)

Needless to say, the young man who came to minister with me no longer believes the age of miracles is over. His sister sent me a message on Facebook afterward, saying, "My brother is the one who helped heal the deaf man with you. He is totally wrecked after that, so thank you for being so awesome."

Jesus is and always will be the same, yesterday, today and forever. That description of *awesome* is an acknowledgment of Christ's identity shared with us. He is awesome. And He is in us!

Will You Increase the Power?

We have talked about the fact that God created human beings to reign over the world He created. But we cannot learn to rule without being in sync with Him. Ruling comes from knowing and living your true identity. It comes not through do's and don'ts but in the grace of being.

If you are a parent, think about how you have taught your children to rule over certain aspects of their lives. When they first came into the world, you had to do everything for them. Then you showed them how to do things for themselves, like brushing their teeth and making sure their shoes are on the right feet. Eventually, you gave them control over dressing themselves. This may not always have been pretty at first. They did not understand that a top with vertical stripes does not go with checked pants. But with your patient instruction, they eventually got better at it.

As they demonstrated responsibility in that area of life and continued to grow, you expanded their responsibilities by allowing them to rule over their bedrooms. As you instructed them and worked beside them, they learned how to make their beds, put up their toys and keep things orderly and neat. And so it goes until they grow up and reach the point of being ready to go out into the world on their own.

The same is true in our life with God. We need to grow up in our ability to rule and reign over more and more aspects of life God gives to us. And we need to demonstrate we can take on such responsibility.

It is like the Parable of the Talents that Jesus tells in Matthew 25. A rich man goes on a journey and leaves three of his servants to look after his wealth. One man receives five bags of gold, another receives two bags and a third receives only one.

When the master returns from his journey, he discovers the first two servants have both invested and doubled what he entrusted to them. The third man took his bag and buried it so that he was able to return the exact amount left to him.

The rich man told the first two servants, "You have been faithful with a few things; I will put you in charge of many things" (Matthew 25:21). But he was angry with the servant who had not used what was entrusted to him.

What I learn from this is that God expects us to use the talents and gifts He has given us. The Identity Thief, on the other hand, wants us to bury our talents in the dirt and act like "normal" people.

Yet Jesus calls us to be extraordinary. Elsewhere in the gospels, He says:

> "Go into all the world and preach the gospel to all creation. Whoever believes and is baptized will be saved, but whoever does not believe will be condemned. And these signs will accompany those who believe: In my name they will drive out demons; they will speak in new tongues; they will pick up snakes with their hands; and when they drink deadly poison, it will not hurt them at all; they will place their hands on sick people, and they will get well."
>
> Mark 16:15–18

This is the normal Christian life—and it is ours, so long as we stay plugged in to the Power Source. As we step out in faith, He will enlarge our abilities and gifts to the point where we will be able to see the lame walk, the blind see and, yes, even the dead rise!

Through the Parable of the Talents, Jesus gives us permission to explore the height, depth and width of authority and power He reinstated to us at the cross. Jesus is saying through this parable, "Go get it, and see what is waiting for you."

Be reckless! Be bold! Every victory you achieve will give you faith for the next, bigger victory. And every failure will give you the experience and strength you need not to give up but to try again and grow.

6

UNMASK SATAN

But if we are living in the light of God's presence, just as Christ does, then we have wonderful fellowship and joy with each other, and the blood of Jesus his Son cleanses us from every sin.

1 John 1:7 TLB

Scott and his wife were faithful members of a church I pastored. They were an attractive couple in their mid-twenties who loved Jesus and were heavily involved in church activities. They were young, enthusiastic and quick to lend a hand when one was needed. In short, they were just the sort of people every church needs.

Many of the members of our church had come from difficult backgrounds. Some had been in gangs. Others had overcome addictions to drugs and alcohol. Some had been homeless and struggling to survive on the streets. But Jesus had reached down and pulled them out of the darkness and into the light of His magnificent love.

I did not know much about Scott's past, but it seemed he and his wife were attracted to our church because they felt a connection with our community and a sense of safety somehow. What I did know is that his future looked bright.

Then one day after one of our worship services, he pulled me aside and asked if he could talk to me in private.

"Of course," I said.

As soon as the sanctuary was empty, I led him back to my office and offered him a seat.

"What's on your mind?" I asked.

He squirmed a bit, clearly considering how to say what he wanted to tell me. After a moment or so, he just blurted it out.

"Everybody calls me Scott," he said, "but I'm not Scott."

I was not sure I had heard him right. "What do you mean?" I asked.

"I'm not Scott," he repeated. "Scott is dead."

Now he really had my attention.

"Scott is the name of a guy who's dead," he explained. "He was my age. We grew up in the same area. But my life was so bad that I decided the only thing to do was change my identity. So . . ."

"You assumed Scott's identity."

He nodded. "I needed a new start, and I didn't know what else to do. I did things that were so horrible that if the authorities found me, I would be put away for a long time. My wife doesn't even know who I really am. She only knows Scott. She has no clue that the name she took isn't mine."

About that time, his wife called into the office, looking for him. "Scott?" I heard her say.

He shook his head and sighed. "It's not me. I'm living a lie. Nobody knows who I really am."

I wish I could say this story has a happy ending. Unfortunately, it does not. It would not prove easy for Scott to get untangled from the mess he had gotten himself into. There were consequences, and he was not willing to face them. He continued wearing a mask and pretending to be someone else.

The Identity Thief loves this. He loves it when we keep our true selves hidden from the world. We cannot have a true relationship with people who do not know who we really are. But there is a tremendous power that comes from living in complete honesty when we share with others who we really are. This is the only way we can get back to being the salt and light God intends us to be.

Scott saw light in us at the church. It spoke life to him, but it also exposed the false life he was living. In coming to me, he was saying, "Help me be the true self God made me to be."

He had only to step out and do it. Unfortunately, he could not find the strength to do so.

A Life of No Disguises

Before I get further into this, I want to point out one of the things Scott did that was absolutely right on. We all make a mess of our lives. We all need a fresh start. The only way to get it is to take on the identity of a dead man. Of course, I am talking about Jesus Christ, who died on the cross to give us forgiveness of sins and cleanse us from all unrighteousness.

We have become new creations, as Paul writes in 2 Corinthians 5:17: "Therefore, if anyone is in Christ, the new creation has come: The old has gone, the new is here!" He also writes, "I have been crucified with Christ and I no longer live, but Christ lives in me. The life I now live in the body, I live by faith in the Son of God, who loved me and gave himself for me" (Galatians 2:20).

Jesus gives all of us a chance to start over. But He does not give us a disguise to wear. Rather, He sets us free to be who we truly are—who God always intended us to be. I wish the same could be said of Scott's choice.

It is absolutely vital to keep walking forward in the freedom Jesus has given us. Tragically, Christians do not always do that. They fall by the side because the Identity Thief knows where we are weakest, and that is where he hits us. Some are tempted by the thrill of illicit sex, others by their desire for power, money or reputation.

From time to time, I have people tell me they will never set foot in a church because they have known Christians who were hypocrites. Whenever I hear that, I think, *But there are probably a lot of hypocrites at your favorite restaurant. Does that keep you from going there to get a tasty meal?* Neither should it keep us from going to church to understand and encounter our true selves.

Besides, I have a feeling a lot of people we might think are hypocrites really are not. These are people who truly feel a calling to live for Jesus. That is what they want to do. But they have fallen victim to the Identity Thief. This does not make them hypocritical when they sit in church, praising God, because that is their true identity. That is who they really are. When they engage in behavior of the sin nature, that is when they wear a mask. That is when they are hypocritical. Satan is the one who is all about the masks. He keeps us from our true identity. He keeps us living inside lies.

A Life Meant for Freedom

Satan is sneaky in his tactics. We have to be on guard at all times or else we run the risk of slipping into his system of wearing masks.

That is what happened to my dad after many years of serving Jesus. After all the good he did, he went through a season of being trapped by the Identity Thief. In fact, he would be the first one to tell you he is a good example of what can happen when we allow Satan to deceive us into thinking it is okay to hide who we really are. We cannot. Nor can we keep hidden from God.

Before I go further in this story, it is important that you know that my dad and I have a very good and close relationship. We have butted heads many times—it is a Dawkins thing to do—but I would say we are best friends. I also want you to know that my parents were both wonderful people who loved the Lord with all their hearts. From the time he was a young man, my dad had a passion for telling others about Jesus. He was a powerful, persuasive speaker who won hundreds, perhaps thousands, of people to Christ.

You already know my parents were missionaries in Japan when I was born. My earliest memories are all related to church ministry. That is how my sisters and I spent quality time with our parents. I could not have been more than four or five years old when my parents formed a family music group called Bob, Rose and the Buds to spread the good news about salvation through Christ. (My dad's name was Bob and my mother was Rose. My sisters and I were the Buds.) We performed at Kiwanis club meetings and fairs and even appeared on some television shows.

My dad was an entrepreneur who always had something big going on. None of his schemes were ever intended to gain personal wealth. Everything he did was designed to enlarge the borders of God's Kingdom. And for a long time, it seemed everything he put his hand to prospered.

For example, after we returned from Japan, my family got involved in a ministry that had formed from a home Bible study in Dallas, Texas, that quickly evolved into a Christian community and a Bible school. One of my dad's roles as public relations director for the international ministry was recruiting students, and he was really good at it. He had a gift for motivating people and instilling within them a passion to live for Christ.

At the time, he kept pressing other people in the ministry to start a television station to help spread the Gospel. He also believed Dallas desperately needed a station that would broadcast good, moral programs families could watch together. This must have seemed like a crazy dream to most of my dad's friends. I know what I would say if someone tried to talk me into starting a television station: "Do you have any idea how much that would cost? And what do I know about running a television station anyway?"

As usual, my dad was not deterred. He raised almost all of the money himself, most of it from multimillionaire Christians in the Dallas area. What a happy day it was when KXTX Channel 33 TV went on the air for the first time! Later on, that station would become one of the first local broadcast entities owned by Pat Robertson's Christian Broadcasting Network.

Everything was going well in Dallas. The ministry was growing, the college was full of students and the television station was on the air. People were being won to Jesus every day.

Then the Identity Thief struck.

The main leader of the ministry was tempted into an extra-marital affair. It seemed entirely out of his character. Everyone was shocked when they heard about it. But it happened, and the entire ministry slowly dissolved.

We left Texas for Georgia, where my dad had spent his boyhood.

Now, in addition to having a passion for the Gospel, both of my parents also had a deep love for people of color. Even though my dad was raised in the deep South, he always hated every form of racism, and my mother felt even more passionate about it.

Our church and school were right on the dividing line between the black and white sections of the city. Everything to the north of us was white. Everything to the south was black. My dad was delighted with the church's location, because it gave him the perfect platform from which to take the Gospel into black neighborhoods.

Our location also put us in the center of much racial tension and strife. We experienced pushback and hate from both blacks and whites, but that was a price my parents were willing to pay. My dad had always been a vocal supporter of the civil rights movement, and, as you can imagine, that did not sit well with some of our friends in Atlanta. In fact, our church lost several members because of my dad's stance on race relations. I admire him and my mother for that.

This was in the days before corporal punishment was outlawed, and my mother was the disciplinarian at International Life Corps Academy, the school they started at Baptist Chapel. In 1970, I remember that she paddled about thirty students, mostly white but some black also, for using the N word. My parents just would not tolerate racism—and yes, we lost some students because of it.

One time, my dad took some kids to the Underground in Atlanta. At the time, the Underground was mostly bars and strip clubs. My dad said to my friend Jerry Snyder, "We're going to change paupers into princes tonight. They don't know who they really are. Let's show them tonight."

Before the evening was over, Jerry had brought fourteen people to faith in Jesus. He was hoping for just one.

It was shortly after this that my father forgot who he was in Christ. Just as had happened to the leader of that ministry in Texas, my dad got involved in an extramarital affair. And as soon as that happened, there was a noticeable shift in the ministry. Some people left the church, and things just started to fall apart.

My dad lost the freedom intended for him by God when the Identity Thief tricked him into living a double life—a life of masks.

A Life That Needs Truth

My dad's fall into sin began with a woman who had already seduced another pastor in our city. My dad did not know anything about that, and when she approached him, he fell for it.

It still blows me away and makes my heart ache to see those who have walked with Jesus for years, people like my dad, who care so deeply about the lost and hurting and who have carefully built pristine reputations, lose it all in a moment of weakness. But that is what my father did. He did it even though he and my mother had a healthy relationship. There was no strife between them. But the thrill of the affair was like an adrenaline rush. It was just as Proverbs 9:17 says: "Stolen water is sweet; food eaten in secret is delicious!"

My understanding is that this first affair was a one-time thing. I believe it was a conquest for the woman, that she was someone who took delight in getting pastors to fall into sin.

But the Identity Thief had his hooks in my dad, and there were other affairs to follow.

The years of my dad's affairs were difficult ones for our ministry and our family. It was like we were riding a roller coaster. The church would begin to grow in numbers and spiritual fervor, and then, for no apparent reason (or so we thought), things would take a serious downturn. People would move away. Some would leave for other churches. And we would see our attendance drop radically.

Before my dad fell into sin, there was a joy at Baptist Chapel. The church was full of young people, and it was like we were all in a raft shooting downriver. Everything was easy. After the affair, it was like we were trying to fight our way upstream. Nothing came easy. I remember my dad saying over and over again, "Why can't we get a break?"

I believe now that what was going on at Baptist Chapel mirrored my dad's behavior. From time to time, he would start fasting, praying and trying to extricate himself from his sinful lifestyle. When that happened, the church would begin to prosper. Then he would again fall into temptation, and everything would start to fall apart again. For years, he continued in sin, trying to keep it hidden instead of repenting and allowing God to forgive and restore him. Some people may have been fooled, but God sees everything.

Also, because my dad knew he was not living the life God wanted for him, he began to neglect reading the Bible. His prayer life was not as robust. His sermons were not as dynamic as before. Sometimes it seemed he was not thoroughly prepared to preach. As his spiritual life suffered, the spiritual life of the church suffered as well.

As I look back on those years, I see one of the things my dad did that hurt our church was try to dampen my mom's spiritual gifts. My mother had very strong worship, teaching and prophetic gifts that God used to bless people and bring them closer to Him. But because my dad was not living in his true identity, I think he was somewhat afraid of my mom's prophetic gift. What if God spoke through her and exposed him to the congregation and his family? And so he often cut her short or overlooked her when she had something to say. He was doing something the Bible warns us against. He was "suppress[ing] the Spirit" (1 Thessalonians 5:19 MESSAGE).

This went on for thirteen years or more. It started when I was around seven years old and carried on until I was 21, when my dad confessed his sin with many tears and much anguish to my mom, my sisters, myself and our church. My mother knew what was going on the entire time, yet she never said a word to anyone other than my father. In fact, I never heard my mother say anything bad about anyone. This was part of her godly character.

What happened was the Lord showed my older sister Debbie that something was wrong with one of the women involved with my dad. Debbie sensed the woman was involved in sexual sin and that the Lord was calling her back to the light. When Debbie went to her, the woman confessed to the affair with my father. Debbie then went to my father, and he confessed.

Over the years since, my dad has publicly spoken about his battle with sin. He has used it as an opportunity to talk with men about the importance of sexual fidelity and purity.

Once again, God has brought good out of something the Identity Thief intended for evil.

What I have learned from my dad's mistakes is that it is vitally important to live in the purity Jesus gave us at the cross. When sin tries to creep in, as it will, we must expose the enemy's attempts. We do not need to ask God's forgiveness if we do not act on any of those sinful thoughts. Rather, we must recognize the thoughts as fiery darts shot at us by the Identity Thief. Whenever this happens to me, I typically ask a good Christian friend to pray for me. I might say, "The enemy is really trying to make me slip up. Please be praying for me and fighting with me in prayer so I can turn away from it."

I believe this is what Jesus did, because Scripture says He never sinned but was tempted with every temptation: "For since he himself has now been through suffering and temptation, he knows what it is like when we suffer and are tempted, and he is wonderfully able to help us" (Hebrews 2:18 TLB).

If you have fallen into sin, it is vital to talk to a trustworthy person who will help you get back into the light of God's true identity for you. Remember how Adam and Eve tried to hide from God in the Garden of Eden because they suddenly knew they were naked? The Bible is full of stories about people who tried to hide things from God. It just does not work. God designed us to take off our masks and live in the light of truth.

A Life Free from Masks

So much of the time, the Identity Thief tries to get us to a place of hiding, and then he tries to keep us there. Just like the fig leaves in the Garden of Eden, the masks we wear provide a false sense of obscurity. The leaves were Adam and

Eve's attempt to blend in, to stay hidden, and we use masks the same way today.

When we take off the masks and speak the truth, though, we expose the Identity Thief. Instead of identifying with our sin, we identify with the Savior who makes us redeemed and whole.

Rather than hiding behind masks, I implore you rip off the false image and then step forward and say, "This happened, and I need to speak the truth so I can live in the identity God gave me." This will bring great freedom. It will set you back on the clear path. Discarding your mask is the best thing you can do in the war against the Identity Thief.

7

ENTER THE KILN OF GOD

"For I know the plans I have for you," declares the LORD,
"plans to prosper you and not to harm you, plans to give
you hope and a future."

Jeremiah 29:11

I was holding a conference in the heartland when a woman
in her thirties stood up to share her testimony. None of us
was prepared for her opening sentence.

"My father is a pedophile," she said.

Before we could take that in, she went on to say, "In fact,
all my siblings and I, as well as other children, were sexually abused by my father. He sexually abused us our entire
lives. He taught us how to cover it up so no one else would
find out."

All of us speakers were leaning forward in our seats, thinking, *Oh, no! She has the microphone, and this meeting is really*

going to go south. We had no idea where she was going. But we also knew we could not just stop her after such a startling statement and say, "Thanks for sharing."

I said a silent prayer that God would take the conversation in a direction that would benefit everyone, and I nodded for her to go on.

"I hadn't seen my father for about fifteen years," the woman continued, "but I heard he was in the hospital, about to have major surgery. So after hearing what Robby had to say about true identity, I decided I was going to go to the hospital and see him."

She went on to say that when she got to the hospital, she almost turned around and left. As she stood in the hallway outside her father's room, she could hear him making lewd, suggestive comments to the nurses attending him inside.

"I watched as the nurses came out, sickened and repulsed by all the things he was saying to them." She choked back the lump that had formed in her throat. "I began to feel this repulsion and disgust. Did I really want these nurses to know this horrible man was my dad?"

But she told herself she had come this far and did not want to turn back now. She prayed for strength and courage, and then she strode into his room.

Her father looked up at her and said something like, "Hey, good looking, what are you doing here?" It had been so long, he did not recognize his own daughter.

She walked right over to him and said, "It's me. It's your daughter."

The man's mouth fell open in surprise. She was the last person he had expected to see.

"This is not who you are," she told him. "You're supposed to be a man of God who loves and protects his children, a man who sees his children as a precious treasure. You were created to be a man of God. Now, rise up, man of God. Rise up from this lie you have believed about yourself."

The woman's words penetrated her father's heart, and he began to weep. He knew she was right. He had not lived the identity God had given him. Her words convicted him of his true identity and exposed the sin nature Satan had convinced him to embrace. Right then and there, he accepted Christ at the invitation of the daughter he had violated all those years ago.

As she prayed with him, the woman's feelings toward her father began to soften.

"I grew up hating my father," she told us. "But I began to weep over the man my father should have been and was now becoming."

What will happen to this man and his daughter? Will they be able to build a decent relationship after all these years? I cannot say for certain they will. But I believe that as she sees past the mess he made of his life—and the pain he inflicted on his children—and instead sees him the way God intended him to be, she will help him become that person.

This is about being willing to let the fire of God refine us. Will we let God shape us into the people we were always meant to be, the people we have forgotten we are because the Identity Thief has worked his designs against us for so long? As long as you are still alive, it is never too late to reclaim your Christ-restored identity.

Please know that counseling and emotional healing are also a vital part of the steps ahead for this man and his daughter. That is part of the refining process God uses for our growth, too. God has given great wisdom to professional counselors, who can help bring healing to many internal wounds.

A Fire God Uses

As we talk about entering the kiln of God—the refining fire that burns away everything false the Identity Thief places on us—I want you to know that going through rough times does not mean God has turned His back on you. Rather, He is redemptive, which means He is taking those painful, hard things and turning them back on the enemy by molding and perfecting you into the image of His Son.

I believe that as children of God, we can expect to walk in power and experience miracles on a constant basis. But I would never tell you that you will not go through tough times because you're a Christ-follower. That is just not true. We all must go through the kiln of God to be purified and made ready for service in His Kingdom.

Think about it this way. Clay that has not gone through the fire of the kiln is useless. Fire solidifies clay. It makes clay strong and helps it retain its shape. This is how it works with clay, and this is how it works with people, too.

For example, you could not possibly find a better example of a powerful Christian than the apostle Paul. Consider the power he demonstrated after being shipwrecked on the island of Malta. A poisonous snake bit him on the hand, but he shook it off into the fire.

At first, the people who were watching decided Paul must be a murderer who could not escape justice. They expected him to swell up and die, which was what normally happened when somebody was bitten by a poisonous viper. But when Paul shook the snake into the fire and did not even get a mild fever, they decided he must be a god. The passage goes on to say Paul prayed for all of the sick people on the island and they were cured. (See Acts 28:1–9.)

Despite being a mighty man of faith and power, Paul had more than a few difficult moments along the way. In 2 Corinthians 11, Paul says he was

- Exposed to death again and again
- Given 39 lashes on five separate occasions
- Beaten with rods three times
- Pelted with stones once
- Shipwrecked three times, with a night and a day spent in the open sea
- Deprived of sleep
- Hungry, thirsty, cold and naked

He writes, "I have been in danger from rivers, in danger from bandits, in danger from my fellow Jews, in danger from Gentiles; in danger in the city, in danger in the country, in danger at sea; and in danger from false believers" (verse 26).

Paul spent plenty of time in the kiln of God.

Consider, too, another example from the book of Daniel. Three young men—Shadrach, Meshach and Abednego—were bound and thrown into a super-heated furnace when they refused to bow down and worship a golden idol erected by King Nebuchadnezzar. The king was so outraged that he ordered the furnace to be heated seven times hotter than usual.

The three were bound and tossed into the fire, but they did not burn up. Instead, the king looked into the furnace and saw four men walking around in there. Nebuchadnezzar asked his attendants, "Weren't there three men that we tied up and threw into the fire? Look! I see four men walking around in the fire, unbound and unharmed, and the fourth looks like a son of the gods" (Daniel 3:24–25).

It was only because these three young heroes were thrown into the fire that they encountered the Son of God. The king, too, would never have seen Jesus without the experience of fire. We learn that because of this miracle, King Nebuchadnezzar praises God and commands His name to be revered (see verses 28–29).

The same thing happens to us when we find ourselves in the fire. We may not escape the flames entirely, but God will meet us there, and He promises:

> "When you pass through the waters, I will be with you; and when you pass through the rivers, they will not sweep over you. When you walk through the fire, you will not be burned; the flames will not set you ablaze. For I am the LORD your God, the Holy One of Israel, your Savior."
>
> Isaiah 43:2–3

In the fire, Christ is revealed. If you are going through a difficult, challenging time, look for Jesus. He may not be the source of the struggle, but in its midst He is redemptive and can show Himself powerfully. He can use what you are going through.

A Fire We Can Fight

I even believe God sometimes expects us to run *toward* trouble instead of away from it. Jesus said the gates of hell will not prevail against His Church (see Matthew 16:18). This is a picture of the Church on the offensive, smashing down the gates of the enemy and rescuing those he has taken captive.

Too often, we think of the Church as a fortress, a place to hide from the troubles of the world. Really, it should be more like a war room, where we gain the strength we need to do battle against the enemy.

The fourth chapter of Acts talks about a time when the early Church began to face persecution from the Jewish and Roman authorities. Peter and John had been jailed a short time and were then ordered never to preach in the name of Jesus again. When this was reported to the other believers, they took the matter to God in prayer. But they didn't pray for safety or protection or to be spared from the troubles about to come. Instead, they prayed:

> "And now, O Lord, hear their threats, and give us, your servants, great boldness in preaching your word. Stretch out your hand with healing power; may miraculous signs and wonders be done through the name of your holy servant Jesus."
>
> Acts 4:29–30 NLT

Look how God answers their prayer in verse 31: "The meeting place shook, and they were all filled with the Holy Spirit. Then they preached the word of God with boldness." I believe He was very pleased that as they looked into the flames of persecution, they could see Jesus glorified. Rather than running away, they responded to persecution with strength and boldness.

A Fire We Need

After I found out about my dad's infidelity, I certainly felt like I was in the fire and in need of holy boldness. Here was a man I had respected my whole life. I saw him as a man of faith and conviction. I never suspected he would be unfaithful to my mother—and especially not over any length of time. It would have been difficult enough to think he would fall once, but to know it had happened again and again over such a long period of time was a crushing blow.

To my dad's credit, when my sister confronted him about the situation, he did not deny it or try to lie about it. Instead, he confessed, and then he told the rest of us about it.

As for me, I did not know what to do or where to go. I still lived at home with my mom and dad. I was active in the church, where I served as youth pastor. Being involved in ministry was all I had ever known. It was what God had called me to do. But should I continue at our church after what had happened? How could I continue serving under the authority of a man who had neither godly oversight nor a restoration plan?

I told my dad I was leaving, but he begged me to stay.

"The church needs you," he told me. "The people need you. You're doing such a good job."

I was torn, because I did love the few kids and families I had worked with, and I did not want to walk off and leave them without a leader.

When my dad's compliments did not work, he tried another approach.

"I'm worried about what will happen to you if you leave the ministry," he told me. "You've been here in this safe, beautiful environment—and I'm afraid you might go off the deep end."

He told me stories about people he knew who had made a wrong turn in life and wound up addicted to drugs, homeless or in jail. He did not want the same thing to happen to me.

The sad thing was that I believed him. I did not have a clear understanding of who I was in Christ. I did not know my identity.

I needed some time to think, so I called my sister and asked if I could spend the weekend with her.

"Of course," she said. "You know you're welcome here."

I also went to see a counselor at one of the bigger charismatic churches in the Atlanta area. God blessed me by allowing me to talk to a kind, compassionate, wise pastor there. He listened to me for three-and-a-half hours while I unpacked my story.

At the end of our session, he said, "Everything I'm hearing you say is that you need to leave. But you're looking for somebody to give you a directive. I think that's what you want me to do, but I can't do that. If I did, I'd just be replacing the role of your father. It sounds to me like he's been telling you what to do your whole life. But again, it also sounds to me like it's time for you to make that move."

When the weekend was over, I went home and told Dad I was leaving.

But he just shook his head.

"Why don't you take some time to fast and pray about it?" he offered. "I'll have someone cover your duties, and if you come out of that time thinking you still should leave, I'll bless you. I'll even help you get a new start. I know—why don't you lock yourself in the church for a few days? You'll have a bathroom there. Water. And there's juice in the refrigerator."

It sounded like a good idea to me. There could not possibly be a better place than a church for seeking God. So I packed my Bible, my concordance and a notebook and locked myself into the sanctuary. Over the next 72 hours, I spent a lot of time seeking God's direction. To be honest, I also spent a lot of time sleeping on my bedroll on the sanctuary floor. It was the first real break I had taken in years, and I was exhausted. For obvious reasons, I was also emotionally spent.

I cannot say God spoke to me and told me what to do. At that time, I would not even know what that could be like. But the more time I spent in prayer, the more I was convinced God was calling me to move on. I just could not stay on in my dad's ministry any longer. Things felt lifeless, visionless, and I could not pretend and just go on with business as usual.

I also knew I had hit a serious ceiling. I felt my dad had cut out so much of my mother's powerful ministry, and I felt his dominant personality would stifle me as well. The youth pastor role was extremely limited and hindered. It was not going to be easy, but I would have to tell him the time had come for me to leave.

Early in the morning of my third day of prayer and fasting, my dad dropped by the church to see if I had heard from God.

I swallowed hard and said, "Dad, I just feel confirmed that I'm supposed to leave."

His eyes narrowed and he asked, "Can you give me a Scripture for that?"

I was not sure what he wanted. I could show him many Scriptures that talked about what he had done, but no, God had not given me a specific Scripture that said something like, "I want you to leave, Robby." All I could share with him was that I was clearly getting in my spirit that it was time for me to go.

He put his arm on my shoulder.

"Well, son, think about what it was like for Joseph when he was in prison," he said. "Even though he may have felt that all was lost, he was right where God wanted him to be—and on the road to where God wanted him to go. So, based on that, I believe God is telling you that you need to stay."

I could not believe what I was hearing. But instead of re-acting in anger, I broke down and began weeping, because I realized my dad was not living up to his agreement with me.

He was not honoring his word to let me go if I felt certain that was what God wanted me to do. This wounded me.

I stayed a couple more months, but then more allegations of sexual infidelity arose, which my dad had no choice but to admit.

Of course, by this time, I knew my dad had been involved in sexual immorality. But now I was seeing the full extent of what had happened. Furthermore, it became clear to me that my dad had not really put his sins behind him. I think he was hoping everything would blow over and we would move on like we did last time. But this time, the woman stayed in the ministry and did not leave like the previous one had.

A meeting was called to discuss the fallout of this latest indiscretion. It was in the middle of this meeting with me, my mom, my dad and two other church leaders that I decided I could not stay any longer. This new fire finally gave me the strength to leave a place I needed to leave.

"Dad," I said, "you just won't change. You haven't repented. It breaks my heart, but I can no longer be a part of this."

With tears in my eyes, I got up and walked out of the church.

"You come back here right now!" my dad called after me, his angry voice echoing off the walls.

But this time, I was not going to give in. I kept on walking.

A Fire That Gifts

When my dad realized I was not coming back, he gave me a set of carpet-repair tools and some equipment to do industrial-strength carpet cleaning. As I mentioned, my dad was an entrepreneur who had his hand in a number of businesses, and carpet cleaning was one of them. In helping me, I believe he felt a sense of responsibility, seeing how much of my life had been given to serving under him and surrendering my life to his purpose and vision. I had hoped he might try to open doors for me to get involved in ministry somewhere else, but at least this was something.

I spent the next few months living with my sister Ella and her husband. Ella had always been a support system for me. She had a tender heart like my mother, and I always felt safe with her. Her husband had a job with a carpet-cleaning service, and he and another friend helped me get a job there. At least I had a way to make a living. My sister also allowed me to use a car to get to work.

I started attending another church in the area—Atlanta Christian Center—and what a great experience that was! The church was full of healthy families. Sure, they had issues. Everybody does. But they loved each other and supported each other. They modeled the way Christ-followers should treat each other.

I realized then that because of the situation at my dad's church, I had been starving spiritually. It is not that my dad was not a strong speaker and an excellent leader. He was. But my dad—and thereby the entire church—was operating under a cloud of sin that blocked God's grace. Had he truly repented and turned away from his sin, I believe the glory of God would have returned, and with great force. But he did not, and it did not. We often think God puts us under judgment when we err, but I believe what happens is we pull ourselves out from under His grace.

My mother always spoke truth to my father but never nagged him. She would separate from him for a month or so and then come back. This continued for several years, until my father finally told the other woman she had to leave. Yes, even after coming clean about the affair, he kept the other woman around. By the time the woman left, his ministry had dwindled to three people. Their church was a ghost town. He never recovered in ministry.

Everything I am doing today, my father should have been doing. I am truly living his dream.

I learned an important lesson from this. If you want to grow as a Christ-follower and become all you are capable of being, then you need to be in a place where you are getting spiritually nurtured.

Now, I have got to say that I do not believe in church-hopping. I have known people who would go from church to church to church. Every time they thought they had found a church home, something happened that offended them, and they left. I believe it is important to find a good church home and hang in there. There is no such thing as a perfect church. People need a lot of grace. But if you are not getting anything out of it and you feel like you are stagnating, then it is probably time to move on.

As I mentioned earlier, when you are in the fire of your difficult experience, look for Jesus. When I was struggling through the realities of my father's sin, I could have lost faith completely. But in the midst of that experience, I saw my mother clinging to her relationship with Jesus as never before. I was so inspired by her devotion that it made me press into Him like never before, too.

This is why we need the church. Even amidst abusive leaders who are not following Jesus as they should, we can find balance in relationship other places. My encouragement is that you increase your personal relationship with Christ and find similar Christ-followers to befriend. Walk together and watch together for the ways Christ is loving, strengthening and supporting you—even in the fires of His love.

8

STAND IN THE TRUTH

Coming to his hometown, he [Jesus] began teaching the people in their synagogue, and they were amazed. "Where did this man get this wisdom and these miraculous powers?" they asked. "Isn't this the carpenter's son? Isn't his mother's name Mary, and aren't his brothers James, Joseph, Simon and Judas? Aren't all his sisters with us? Where then did this man get all these things?" And they took offense at him. But Jesus said to them, "A prophet is not without honor except in his own town and in his own home."

Matthew 13:54–57

If you are determined to walk in spiritual integrity, there will be times you have to speak up when you would rather keep your mouth shut. And when you do speak up, people will not always agree with you. You may even find yourself at odds with other believers you love and respect. But that is okay, because you will be in really good company. Skim through the Old Testament and see how poorly they treated the prophets in those days. And remember what Jesus said:

> "Blessed are you when people insult you, persecute you and falsely say all kinds of evil against you because of me. Rejoice and be glad, because great is your reward in heaven, for in the same way they persecuted the prophets who were before you."
>
> Matthew 5:11–12

Here is how I learned this.

Stepping Out

Although I loved attending Atlanta Christian Center, I decided to go one Sunday to visit the church my sister attended in another city. This church was huge. It had several thousand members, an international media ministry and a pastor who was a well-known charismatic leader. It was a long drive for me, but I thought I would check it out.

Almost from the time I walked through the door, I was treated like somebody special. It was as if the people there immediately recognized the talents and abilities God gave me. There was even some talk about my joining the staff someday. This excited me because I knew full-time ministry was where God called me to be. And even though I was giving everything I possibly could to the other congregation, nobody there ever said anything to me about getting a staff position. Of course, to be fair, the megachurch had lots and lots of staff positions. Name just about anything you can think of, and they probably had an assistant pastor in charge of it.

There was a big problem for me, however, in that I felt guilty about leaving the other church. Because of what I had been through at my dad's ministry, I did not understand it was possible to move on in a healthy, positive way. I figured the people in the other church would be upset with me for leaving, no matter what my reasons might be, so I left without a word.

It was not long before the pastor started calling me to make sure I was okay and to find out what had happened to me. He must have left fifteen messages, but I ignored them all. I just knew he was going to yell at me, and I did not want to deal with that.

Then one evening, he called five or six times in a row. Almost as soon as the phone stopped ringing, it started ringing again. Realizing he was not going to give up, I finally answered.

As I expected, his voice sounded curt and almost angry. He asked me where I had been, if I was okay and so forth.

Instead of calmly answering his questions, I burst into tears.

"I'm sorry," I cried. "I know you hate me, and I don't blame you. I know you think I'm ungodly and that I'm going to end up on drugs . . ."

"What?" he said. "Wait a minute—what are you saying? I don't hate you! What are you talking about?"

In an instant, his voice went from clipped and curt to apologetic and concerned.

"Robby, this is going in a direction I didn't expect," he said. "I don't think any of those things. I don't know what you're talking about."

We talked for a few more minutes, and I told him that although I loved Atlanta Christian Center, I felt my future lay with the other congregation.

He asked if we could get together to talk about things, but I said no. I figured if I met with him in person, he was going to tell me I had made the wrong decision and basically treat me the way my dad did.

He ended up telling me if I felt God calling me to the other church, that was where I should go. But he also said he was disappointed because he had envisioned big things for me and had looked forward to having me on his staff someday. If he had told me that before, I might have stayed. But by this time, I was already getting plugged in with the new congregation.

As it turned out, I might have been better off if I had stayed at Atlanta Christian Center. But I am also glad I did not for two very important reasons. The first, and most important to me, is that it was at the new congregation that I met my future wife, Angie. I cannot imagine where I would be today without this beautiful, strong and fearless woman, my best friend and partner in ministry.

The second reason is that I still had some important lessons to learn about what happens when people submerge their spiritual identity in "groupthink" and refuse to question what must be questioned. I often pray that God will help me to be open-minded without being gullible, discerning without being critical. It is not good to be one of those people who question everything. But neither does God expect us to accept everything we are told without questioning anything at all. And that is something I needed to learn.

The truth is, there were a lot of things going on at this new church that should have been questioned, but nobody seemed to be paying attention. God used my experience there to grow me up in this new way I needed to learn.

Noticing Signs

Over the next few weeks and months, I made myself as valuable at the new church as I possibly could. Although I was still working for the carpet-cleaning company, I also spent a lot of time at the church, volunteering wherever I was needed. And just as I had hoped, it was not long before I took a full-time job in the church's television ministry. As God planned it, that was also where Angie worked, and we soon became good friends.

Angie was one of the first people I met when I started attending the new church, but never in a million years would I have expected us to wind up together. She was absolutely beautiful. But she also impressed me as someone who was very tightly wound. I did not know why, but I felt something was not quite right. It was not until much later that God helped me realize He was speaking to me through this impression so I could be a channel of His mercy and grace to her.

I admired Angie for a lot of reasons. She loved God. She was extremely bright and a hard worker. She was beautiful. But I could tell there was something inside her that was wounded and hurting.

We went on one date, actually, but it was a disaster. One of our bosses invited us to go with him and his family to spend the day at a water park. He was trying to set us up, but it did not work well. Later on, when we compared notes, we both thought it was the worst date we had ever been on. Of course, I have to admit I had not dated that many girls, so for me to say it was a bad date did not mean all that much. But Angie had probably dated 25 guys or more. For me to rank right up there as the worst date of all time in her book really said something about how bad that date was.

Now, when I tell you Angie had dated so many guys, I do not want you to get the wrong idea. She had a very high moral standard, and if anyone tried to cross the line with her, that was all she wrote—she was through with them and would not give them a second chance. For this reason, she had a reputation for being a bit of a heartbreaker. Really, she was not. She was a godly woman looking for a man who held the same high standards. And at this church, such a man was not easy to find.

I was surprised by how many of the guys I knew at the church talked casually about sex. I remember one guy saying he had to find a girlfriend because his sex life was really hurting. I thought, *Sex life? You're not even married. You're not supposed to have a sex life.* I could not understand how people who loved the Lord and wanted to serve Him could be so lax in this area of their lives, especially when the Bible's teaching on the subject is so clear. Sex is meant only as a blessing for biblical marriage. Paul says, "Run from sexual sin! No other sin so clearly affects the body as this one does. For sexual immorality is a sin against your own body" (1 Corinthians 6:18 NLT).

Even though I could see a lot of sexual sin going on at the church, I started to make excuses for it. I told myself, *Well, these are modern times. You've got to relax the rules a little to appeal to more people.* I knew couples who were living together without the benefit of marriage, but they were members of the church in good standing. I never heard any sermons on the subject of sexual purity.

People on staff would also make sexual jokes. Men would make suggestive comments about women who were not their wives, and that really bothered me. I began to dabble in some of this coarse jesting myself. Whereas before I had known it was wrong, my standards began to drop.

Speaking Truth

As we worked together, Angie and I began going to lunch together from time to time and building a close friendship. I had gone to her home a few times and enjoyed hanging out with her and her family.

On one occasion, after we had eaten lunch together, I spoke the first prophetic word God had ever given me. I looked at her and said, "I think there's something terribly wrong. I see pain inside of you. You seem tightly wound, and sometimes I even think you could be suicidal. My sense is that the enemy is really seeking to derail you in your life."

I also told her I had an impression that some long-term abuse was in the picture causing her to feel this way.

Upon hearing this, Angie exhaled deeply. It was like watching a balloon deflate. She shook her head.

"It's all true," she said, "but what do I do?"

I told her I did not know, that I just felt the Lord had shown me this, that He loved her and wanted her to get the healing she needed and deserved.

"I just don't know what to do," she responded. "Nobody knows about this. I've never spoken to anyone about it."

The danger of the abuse was still present in her life.

I asked Angie if I could pray for her, and she said of course—even though this was something that was not done very often in this congregation. There was a strong hierarchy in place there, and you were expected to follow set procedures. If you needed prayer, you were supposed to go to the pastor who was assigned to you, and he or she would pray for you. But I could see the agony and pain Angie was carrying, and I wanted to pray for her right then. I could also see how relieved she was that God had revealed this to me. I think that for the first time, she had hope she could overcome the situation.

My concern for Angie opened her heart to me over the next several months. She began to see me as a safe person. Many months after that, she called one night and said, "You know, I really feel like you and I should be an item." (That was the terminology we used back in those days.)

Inside, I started jumping up and down with joy, but I did not let it show.

"Well, why don't we pray about that over the weekend?" I asked.

I could tell her feelings were hurt.

"I don't need to pray about it," she said. "I know."

"Well, let's at least pray about it overnight," I said.

She agreed this was a good idea.

Of course, the next morning, I went to her office and told her that after praying about it, I felt she was definitely someone I would like to be with and that I looked forward to getting to know her better and seeing our relationship grow.

If I have not made it clear enough already, Angie was an exceptionally talented and beautiful woman. She was an extraordinary person and leader, with an IQ so high it was off the charts. She was extremely well read, with a vocabulary that often sent me to the dictionary to make sure I knew what she was talking about. She was good for me in so many ways.

To illustrate the type of person Angie is, after we had officially been "an item" for a couple of weeks, she asked me if we could avoid having physical contact. Now, there had not been much physical contact between us to begin with. We held hands once in a while. I put my arm around her sometimes. And we kissed each other good-night only twice. She wanted to dispense with all of that for a time.

I was shocked, wondering if I had come on too strong. I told her my two strongest love languages were words of affirmation and physical touch, so it might not be easy for me to stop using those means of trying to show her how much I cared about her.

She understood but said, "I need to know our relationship isn't about just the physical stuff. I need to know you love me and that you're not just interested in a physical relationship." Once again, Angie impressed me with her maturity and wisdom. She was absolutely right. We put the physical aspects of the relationship aside and concentrated on getting to know each other better.

I realize now Angie's attitude was connected to the abuse she had suffered. I am not sharing the details of that abuse for obvious reasons. I will say, though, that I urged her to talk to a pastor about what was afflicting her. As a youth pastor myself, once I knew some of the details of the situation, I knew that what had happened to Angie legally had to be reported to the state authorities. But the pastor she approached—a middle-aged single woman—shrugged it off with, "You're probably just not strong enough to handle something like this." That was the only advice Angie got. I was appalled.

Losing Trust

As time went by, Angie and I became more and more close. We were falling in love with each other, and we wanted everyone to be happy about it. Unfortunately, that was not the case.

Before we began dating, Angie had dressed in a more provocative style. She wore tight pants and miniskirts, clothes that accentuated her beautiful appearance. There was nothing unusual about this. At this church, women who did not dress the way Angie did were looked down upon as old-fashioned and frumpy. But after we had been dating for a while, Angie realized she did not need to show off her body.

She was an intelligent, caring, lovely person—and I was happy to see her living in agreement with the Bible's words:

> Don't be concerned about the outward beauty of fancy hairstyles, expensive jewelry, or beautiful clothes. You should clothe yourselves instead with the beauty that comes from within, the unfading beauty of a gentle and quiet spirit, which is so precious to God.
>
> 1 Peter 3:3–4 NLT

Again, not everyone was happy about the change in Angie. From the very beginning of our relationship, the Identity Thief was trying very hard to pull us apart.

The same pastor who had mocked her for not being strong enough to handle the abuse issue called her into the office and told her, "You know, Angie, before you started dating Robby, you were a lot more fun. You dressed fun. You dated a lot of guys. Since you and Robby got together, you just don't come across as fun or even happy anymore."

Angie was incredulous. "What do you mean?" she asked.

"You're kind of dressing like some of the older women," the pastor said. "You used to wear cute miniskirts. You showed cleavage. You need to start being fun again."

Angie could not believe a pastor would give her that kind of advice.

"Well, I saw myself as a different person," Angie tried to explain. "I got my value out of the way I looked. But that's no longer the case."

The pastor smiled a rather condescending smile. "Ah, Angie, it's good for a woman to know that men are looking at her and thinking, 'I wonder what she's got there?'"

As soon as the meeting was over, Angie came straight to my office and told me what had happened. Both of us were astounded.

Gaining Strength

Things did not improve for us when word got around that we were planning to get engaged. One Sunday morning after church, one of the pastors—a married man with children—gave Angie a hug and said, "Concerning Robby, you need to keep your options open."

"What do you mean?" Angie asked.

"You just need to keep your options open."

Angie turned around to walk away, and he called after her, "You're a very pretty girl, and there may be people interested in you that you haven't even considered."

We were told much later this pastor had been involved with many of the young women in the church.

Now, Angie had been attending this church since she was eleven years old. The pastors were more than spiritual leaders to her. They were like her family. As far as she was concerned, they ranked just below God Himself in their authority and wisdom. When they spoke, it was as though they were speaking the oracles of God.

She was bewildered, then, by some of these things that were being said to her. It all seemed so shocking. Could it be that people were trying to protect her? And if so, why? From what?

Even her parents, who had always seemed to like me, started having second thoughts about our getting together. They offered no explanation to me at all; they simply did not want us to see each other.

I was 24 years old, and Angie was 21. She was old enough to decide what she wanted to do, and I knew she was excited to go out with me. But she complied out of fear.

Nobody seemed to care what Angie wanted or thought. Everyone was trying to make up her mind for her. For some reason, there was a tug-of-war going on for her attention and affection.

When word finally got out that we had become engaged, the same pastor from before called us in for a lecture.

"What were you thinking, getting engaged without pastoral permission?" she demanded to know.

"What?" I asked, wondering if I had heard right. "We didn't know we needed your permission."

Angie and I were adults who had the right to get married if we wanted to. And even if we had been kids who needed our parents' permission, my mom and dad would have signed for us right away. My dad and I were back on great terms by this time. He was proud I was still involved in ministry, and he and my mom both thought the world of Angie.

But the lecture from the pastor was not over. Her face red with rage, she said, "Who do you think you are to decide you can get married just like that? We've had our eyes on Angie. We have special plans for her, and now you're ruining everything."

"Special plans?" I asked. "How will our getting married change any of that?"

She could not explain.

Well, in the first place, we had not decided to get married "just like that." We had known each other a couple of years, and we had not even set a date for our wedding yet.

"I need to tell you something," I said to the pastor. "This is wrong. The way you're handling this is wrong, and God won't allow this to happen. You're being abusive to people here."

"You don't know what you're talking about," the pastor snarled.

But we had had enough. We firmly but politely told her so, and then we walked out of her office.

Hearing God

After this, the pressure became intense. I felt as if people were trying to break us up at every turn. Even though I had two roles at the church—one in the media department and one with the youth ministry—it seemed that just about everyone on the church staff was against us. I loved being in ministry, but I felt I had no choice but to resign and go back to working in a secular job. So that is what I did.

A couple nights later, for the second time in my life, I woke to find myself suspended in air. It was 3 a.m., and God was lifting me out of bed and putting my feet on the floor without so much as bending my knees. I was flat on my back in bed and then, *whoosh!* I was standing straight up next to the bed. The feeling was the exact opposite of when the demons had me levitating out of bed when I was in junior high. Then I had felt helpless and terrified, under someone else's control. Now I knew God was waking me up—but for what?

Then I heard a powerful, deep voice command, *Make war!*

"Make war?" I repeated. I did not understand.

Then I felt as if the handle of a sword was thrust into my hand. I started swinging the sword, cutting away at a foe I could not see. I have learned since then that wielding the sword of the Spirit is common practice for some intercessors and charismatic pastors, although I had never heard anything about it until that night.

For three hours, I swung the sword all about me, praying in tongues as I did, and I could feel shackles, ropes and vines that had been wrapped around me being cut away. My spiritual sight was coming clear. The Lord pointed out that in the time I had been at that church, I had stopped praying in tongues. I was not reading the Bible as much as before, and I had quit developing spiritually.

I could sense God's powerful presence in my room. I could also feel angelic beings at war with demonic forces. They were fighting for my freedom. It was powerful!

When I was finished, the Lord took me to the book of Malachi, where He revealed to me that the leaders at this church were abusing His people and that He was calling me to confront it. As I read the book of Malachi, verse after verse jumped off the page. It was like I had been waxed over, just like King Théoden from *The Lord of the Rings*, and now I was coming back to life.

I felt absolutely certain the Lord was telling me the church was struggling with serious issues of adultery, divorce and other sexual sin—and I believed He wanted me to tell the senior pastor what I knew. There was no doubt in my mind he would be shocked to hear what I had to tell him, nor did I doubt he would want to do everything he could to make it right. I could picture him shaking my hand, thanking me for bringing it to his attention, and our becoming prayer partners about it. I hoped a time of repentance and renewal was at hand, to be followed by a great revival.

Confronting Power

Two mornings later, I was in the lobby outside the senior pastor's office, waiting for him at eight o'clock, hoping for a word with him before his first meeting. As I was escorted in, he looked at his watch.

"I've only got a few minutes," he said, obviously not understanding the importance of what I was about to tell him.

"Okay," I said. "Let me just tell you what the Lord said to me."

I read some of the passages from Malachi to him and shared that Angie's abuse had not been properly reported to authorities. I also said that marriages were breaking up and lives were being wounded.

Then I said it straight out. "The Lord has showed me that sexual sin and adultery are rampant in this church, and they need to be dealt with or the whole thing's going to fall apart."

As I talked, the man's eyes grew narrower and his head lowered. He looked angry, but I did not blame him. I knew it must be tough to hear all the things going on in the church he loved and had spent so much of his life building.

But as it turned out, he was not angry about what was happening in the church. He was angry with me for trying to bring it into the light. After I told him what the Lord had shown me, he put his hand up to silence me.

"You listen to me," he said. "You'd better not tell a soul about what you know, or I will completely ruin you. I'll make it to where you can't even be hired as a janitor in a church somewhere."

I shook my head. "I don't understand."

"Everything you're saying is wrong," he said. "But if you tell anyone anything you know, I will ruin you."

"But I don't know anything," I said. "I'm only telling you what the Lord showed me."

"Let me make sure you understand. If you breathe a word of anything you just said or anything you know, I'll make sure you're completely ruined. Do you understand me?"

All I could do was sputter in response as I tried to get my thoughts together. "Well, if what I'm saying is wrong, then why are you threatening me?"

"You listen to me, boy. You don't want to go up against me. You listen to me, and you listen to me good. You'll be ruined, and I mean it. Now, get out of my office."

I stood up to go but felt the Lord stir in me to say something more. "I just have to say this," I said. "If you don't do what the Lord is saying, this place is going to be on every major television network around the country, being exposed for what is going on here, within six months."

"Just go!" the man shouted.

My legs shook as I walked into the lobby. I was devastated. At the same time, I had no doubt I had done exactly what the Lord had impressed upon me to do.

Holding On

Later that week, Angie called and told me she had to break up with me.

"Break up with me?" I asked. "Why?"

It turned out she had been called in to a meeting with one of the pastors, who had talked to the senior pastor, and the pastor had convinced her I was bad for her. If she married me, he said, she would lose her potential. He said I would keep her at home, cranking out babies and watching soap operas, and she would become overweight from sitting on a couch and eating potato chips all day. He was talking like I was some sort of Neanderthal who was going to keep her hidden from the world. "We have better plans for you," the pastor told her.

"That's ridiculous," I told Angie. "What do *you* want?"

"It doesn't matter what I want," she said. "They know what's best for me."

Those were absolutely desperate days for me. I felt I had lost everything dear to me.

By God's grace, Angie called me a few days later and said, "You know, I don't know why I've been listening to these people. You're right. We need to get out of here."

I was overjoyed. I had been fasting and praying that she would see the light.

But while I was delighted by Angie's change of heart, it grieves me to have to tell you nobody at the church listened to the prophetic word the Lord gave me. There was no repentance. No change in leadership. No change in the oppressive, abusive style that had been put in place there.

As a result, scandal broke, just as God said it would. In a matter of months after we finally left, the story was on television stations around the country, and attendance fell by more than 50 percent. It continued to fall over the years to a mere few hundred.

Some of the people who knew what Angie and I had been through at that church asked me if I felt good about what happened there in the end. Absolutely not! My desire is to see every church prosper and grow. As the apostle Paul said:

> It is true that some preach Christ out of envy and rivalry, but others out of goodwill. The latter do so out of love, knowing that I am put here for the defense of the gospel. The former preach Christ out of selfish ambition, not sincerely, supposing that they can stir up trouble for me while I am in chains. But what does it matter? The important thing is that in every way, whether from false motives or true, Christ is preached. And because of this I rejoice.
>
> Philippians 1:15–18

Moving Forward

Despite the way we had been treated at the church, Angie and I felt we were supposed to hang in there a bit longer after the confrontation happened. To leave quickly would be like deserting those who were dealing with the same sort of abuse and frustration we had endured. Certainly, we could not be the only ones abused and mistreated there. We learned later, in fact, we were not the only ones who had tried to confront the issue, but no one in authority paid any attention.

I cannot say it was easy continuing to sit under the ministry of someone who had threatened to ruin me and tear us apart, but Angie and I both felt if this was where God wanted us for a short time longer, we would stay.

Then, in a special New Year's Day service, God gave us a word of prophecy from an unexpected source. During the middle of his sermon, the senior pastor stopped and pointed directly toward the section in the church where Angie and I were sitting.

"You've been saying you can't afford to get married," he said, "but God is saying you can't afford *not* to—and you need to do this soon."

It was like God took over his body for a moment—and then he went back to his sermon.

People all around us were looking at us like, *What was that about?* The statement had nothing at all to do with the rest of what he was talking about in his sermon.

After church that morning, we talked to some friends of ours, Tim and Leandra McHargue, who knew what we had been going through and had been praying for us. They were a lifeline.

"Did anything unusual happen in church this morning?" they asked.

"As a matter of fact, it did," I said.

"Did you get a word from the senior pastor?" Tim asked.

"How did you know?"

They both laughed, and Tim said, "We were praying that God would give you a word through him about getting married today. Robby, the doors of ministry will open back up to you once you and Angie get married."

That is exactly what happened. Angie and I scheduled our wedding for six weeks later, and the day after we returned from our honeymoon, a youth pastor position opened up for me elsewhere.

Even then, though, our trial was not over. Two of the pastors came to us and said, "We heard you guys are in a hurry to get married because Angie is pregnant."

"No way! She's not pregnant!" I cried.

"Well, can you prove it's not true?"

"Wait nine months, and you'll see," was our reply.

For the record, it was a year and a half before our first son was born.

Trusting God

Looking back on that time, it is amazing to see how ruthlessly Satan was trying to steal our identity, both as a couple and as individuals. Through that experience, I discovered there are times other people will not believe in you no matter what you do. If that happens, the only thing you can do is hold your head up straight and understand that it does not matter what other people think about you. What matters is what God thinks about you—and what you know to be true about yourself.

Please know I am not sharing all the details of what transpired during that time. There was so much, and it was truly a hard time. Angie and I have had professional counselors tell us what we went through was the worst personal and spiritual abuse they had ever heard anyone encounter. Many who know our story have told us it is a miracle we continued to be in ministry and an even greater miracle we were still Christians. Many of our dear friends' marriages were destroyed during that time. We saw the faith of so many people decimated, with many becoming atheists afterward. So many lives were ruined.

We held on because we knew that if God was for us, it did not matter who or what was against us—and the same is true for you. You and God are always a majority.

We live as victors, not victims, in this world, even though we have been victimized. After the battle, after we pursue the healing God provides and step back into who we really are, we work to pull others from the debris of their own battles. That is how God does things. He rescues the broken and turns them into rescuers. That is God's revenge against the Identity Thief, and we join Him in it from the place of our true identity.

9

KNOW WHO YOU ARE

I will pour out my Spirit on all people. Your sons and daughters will prophesy, your old men will dream dreams, your young men will see visions.

Joel 2:28

I want to tell you about a dream I had more than twenty years ago, just after God had opened a fresh new door for Angie and me. As I mentioned in the previous chapter, on the day after we returned from our honeymoon, I was hired at a new church as its youth pastor. A short time later, I had this dream.

In the dream, I was in what seemed to be a large gymnasium. Most of the floor area was taken up by an Olympic-sized swimming pool, and there was a smaller, Jacuzzi-sized pool off to the side.

Then I noticed a man I had not seen in at least fifteen years. He had been the leader of the youth group at the church where

I received the powerful word from Iverna Tompkins. You may remember this youth group had experienced an amazing visitation of the Holy Spirit and had spread throughout Atlanta. In just about a month's time, the group went from an average attendance of about thirty kids to over one thousand. So many people were trying to cram into the church that a back wall was knocked out to accommodate everyone.

I was surprised to see this fellow after so many years. I was also surprised to see him because I had never been a part of his youth group. In my dream, he walked up to me, and I asked him, "What are you doing here?"

He did not answer. Then I knew it was the Holy Spirit coming to me in a form I could comprehend.

The man put his hand on my shoulder and said, "Prophesy to the water and tell it to spring to life."

Three times I did as he commanded, prophesying to the Olympic-sized pool, and the water began to bubble up each time. But then it stopped. It was just as had happened in our little church in Atlanta during my boyhood. Baptist Chapel would often seem to catch fire spiritually, but then everything would come to a stop and we would have to start all over.

Then the man pointed at the smaller pool and said, "Now prophesy to this pool."

Again, I did as he commanded. Immediately, a powerful geyser shot up—something like Old Faithful—and when the water hit the floor, it turned into people of all sizes, ages and ethnic backgrounds.

It did not take long for the whole gymnasium to be filled with people—around two thousand of them—all praying for each other. Wide-eyed, I watched as amazing miracles happened all around me. Blind eyes were opened. Bent and twisted limbs were restored. Deadly diseases disappeared.

In the midst of all this, a man stood on a stage. He seemed to be calling out what the Spirit was doing in the room. He was laying his hands on some people, who then went and laid their hands on others, all bringing about mighty healings and miracles. The best way I can describe it is that it was like what happens when you throw a stone into the middle of a pond and watch the ripples move out from the center. Waves of healing were moving out in all directions.

I had never seen anything like it. In my mind, there always had to be a strong leader. He or she was the one the Lord used to do His work. He or she was the conduit for the miracles God gave. I was amazed by the way the "new" people in that gymnasium were ministering to one another, not requiring a leader to do it for them.

Another thing that impressed me was the emotional healing taking place. People were being set free from anger, depression and bitterness—all sorts of emotional pain. Usually, emotional healing takes longer than physical healing. God can heal the body instantly, but it takes longer to heal wounded souls or psyches that have been harmed over years and years.

As I saw all of this happening, I began to weep. I was so moved to see true Body ministry for the first time. Everyone in the room was involved. They were showing the power that belongs to all of us as children of God.

I fell to the ground in the dream and cried out to God, "Lord, I don't understand this. I don't know what this is—but this has to happen."

Then the man who was with me stood me to my feet and told me to look at the person on stage. As I stared at the man on stage, his face became clear, and I saw to my shock and amazement that the man was me. God was calling *me* to do this kind of ministry, to teach it to His people, to show them the power available to all of us who belong to Christ—in other words, to make people aware of their true spiritual identity.

At that point, the floodgates opened and I really began to sob.

"I can't do this!" I cried. "I don't even know what's going on."

Then I began to make all kinds of excuses.

"You've got to find someone else," I said. "I'm not good enough. I'm not capable. But please let this happen. This has to happen."

My companion said, "Look again."

He put his hand on my shoulder, and when he did, I shot up to my feet. This time, the "me" on stage looked at the "me" in the back of the room and called out, "You're the Moses. Don't compromise this."

Then I woke up.

Through tears, I said to God, "I'm not good enough. I can't do this. God, find someone else. But please let this thing happen for people."

Believe What God Tells You

The dream stayed strong with me the next few months. I was never able to push it out of my mind as I went about my new job. Every time I thought about it, I felt a strange mixture of excitement and sadness—excitement over what I had seen the Holy Spirit doing in my dream and sadness because I was being called to do something far beyond my capabilities.

Then on April 25, 1993, a pastor visiting from Florida named Dan White spoke to our congregation. I had never met him before, and I had not told him anything about the dream God had given me. But he gave me a prophecy that day that confirmed what I saw in the dream and helped me know God's response to my fears about it. He said the words of God to me were these:

My son, many have looked at you and said, "What's the use?" Many have said, "Ah, there is nothing to it!" But I say greatness lives in your belly; greatness lives in your bones; a heritage of my righteousness lives within your feet and your legs. I say to you that great will be your latter days. Strong will be your ministry. Don't look to others. Look only to Me, for I am your source. I am your ability. I am your God!

I say unto you the things that have been burning in the pit of your belly—that you've been saying, "God, I can't! God, I can't!" [I am] saying to you, "Release it! Release it! Let it go!" For now is the time for the voice of My Spirit to come forth out of you. Now is the time for the unction of your innermost being to be coming out.

Young ones will run from sin and run to holiness. Darkness will break from around them. Demons will run screaming at your very presence as you step out, because you are My very chosen. . . . I have built you to be a great stronghold for My Kingdom against the enemy. . . . I will use you to keep My little ones from straying away from Me till they are developed and discipled. Disciple them well, My son, for they will bear the image that I have placed in you all around the world.

Yes, I told you that I will raise up apostles, prophets, evangelists and send forth teachers and pastors out of your ministry. You told Me, "God, You're going to have to do it!" Well, I am doing it! I am doing it! I am doing it!

Know this, that I am well pleased. . . . Know that I joy in what you are doing and will do on My behalf. Never forget My hand is not slack, My arm is not short, and My strength has not waned. But I will accomplish that which I have spoken to you in the early morning hours, where you sat before Me weeping in your heart over what I showed you, saying, "God, I can't. God, I'm not good enough. God, find another!"

Then Dan grabbed my shoulders, shook me and shouted God's final words to me, which were, "You are the Moses! Lead My people! Stand strong! And don't compromise that which I have put in your heart!"

After hearing this prophecy, I dropped to the ground like a rock and began to tremble and weep. I find it hard to describe all the emotions that coursed through me when I heard those words: *joy* to think God wanted to use me in such a powerful way; *fear* because part of me still felt God expected more of me than I could possibly deliver; *amazement* that God cared that much about me and had seen me crying on my bed, asking Him to send someone else; and *excitement* because I could not wait to see how God would fulfill this prophecy in my life.

Guard the Truth God Gives You

Of all the emotions bouncing around in me after receiving that prophecy, pride was most definitely not one of them. If God had chosen me to do something special for His Kingdom, it was entirely due to His grace and not any particular strength of mine. In fact, if there had been any pride, it would have been knocked out of me when I reported to the church for work on Monday morning.

There, the senior pastor—my boss—was waiting for me.

"Robby, can I see you in my office for a minute?" he asked.

He wore a big smile, so I had no idea what was about to happen. He invited me to take a seat, then sat behind his desk, intertwined his fingers and said, "That was quite a word you got yesterday, wasn't it?"

I shook my head in amazement. "I was really blown away," I answered.

Then the smile left his face and he leaned forward. "I don't want you to get any wrong ideas here."

"I'm sorry?"

He pointed at me. "You're not the Moses. I'm the Moses!"

"Yes, sir, I understand."

"I'm the leader here, and you'd better not forget it."

I raised my hands in protest. "I don't know where that prophecy came from," I said. "It surprised me every bit as much as it surprised you. Yes, I understand. You're the spiritual leader here."

Now, I loved this pastor. He was a good man struggling through the sort of difficult times all of us experience sometimes. Even so, it took some time to convince him I would never plot against his authority.

My point in sharing this story with you is to let you know that when you respond to fulfill your spiritual identity, there will always be some who try to hold you back and keep you in your place. The source of their attempt is the Identity Thief. He will try to convince them you are prideful and arrogant and that they need to cut you down to size, as this pastor did to me. Do not let the Identity Thief hold you back, and do not let him use others to hold you back, either. If someone is jealous of you for any reason, that is their problem and not yours. You do what the Lord has called you to do, and then watch Him work.

I think my senior pastor got it all wrong that day, anyway. He may have thought God was calling me to a big, new leadership role, but I felt God was saying, "I want you to get the ball rolling. Then give it away—and keep giving it away."

Remember God Is King

Besides, the truth is that God does not need a king. He *is* the king. What He needs is for ordinary people like you and me to step out in faith and be channels of His love and power.

When Saul was chosen to be the first king of the nation of Israel, it was not because God decided His people needed a king. Just the opposite, in fact. The people insisted on having a king because they wanted to be like the other nations that surrounded them. God alone was their king, and He told his prophet Samuel:

> "Listen to all that the people are saying to you; it is not you they have rejected, but they have rejected me as their king. As they have done from the day I brought them up out of Egypt until this day, forsaking me and serving other gods, so they are doing to you. Now listen to them; but warn them solemnly and let them know what the king who will reign over them will claim as his rights."
>
> 1 Samuel 8:7–9

God never needed a king. His goal was always that the greatest of all would be the servant of all (see Matthew 23:11). He is a foot-washing God (see John 13:1–17), a Being who is no respecter of persons and One whose truth is that "there is neither Jew nor Gentile, neither slave nor free, nor is there male and female, for you are all one in Christ Jesus" (Galatians 3:28).

God has never been about hierarchy. He is about yielded hearts and people who are willing to step out in faith because they discover who they are in Christ.

Remember that the Holy Spirit is not controlled by human beings. When Nicodemus came to the Lord at night, Jesus told him, "The wind blows wherever it pleases. You hear its sound, but you cannot tell where it comes from or where it is going. So it is with everyone born of the Spirit" (John 3:8). The Holy Spirit goes where He wants to go and does what He wants to do. He gives miracles where He chooses. He provides healing of body, soul and mind. He is available to all who seek Him in sincere humility. If you belong to Jesus Christ, access to the ministry of the Holy Spirit is part of your spiritual DNA.

This should affect the way you pray. Maybe you can relate to this, but when I first started praying for people to be healed, I sometimes prayed an extra long time. I was not in a hurry to get to "Amen" because I was afraid they would say, "I really don't feel any different." Then I discovered prayer is not powerful because of the one doing the praying. Prayer is powerful because of the One who is in us and the authority He has given us. I do not have to have confidence in myself. My confidence is in Him. And often it is the case that my simplest prayers get the best results.

The same is true for you. As was told to the apostle Paul, "My power is made perfect in weakness" (2 Corinthians 12:9). God is strong in us who are weak. That's the Gospel.

Know God Will Do It

We have talked before about some of the heroes of the Bible who accomplished great things for God even though they did not believe in themselves—Moses, Gideon, Isaiah. Another comes to mind who had a different kind of problem. He believed in himself and knew God had called him to do great things, but nobody else believed him. I am talking about a punk named David.

Did I say punk? Absolutely. Really, that is what most people thought of him—especially his brothers.

For instance, we know David was the greatest king in Israel's history—not counting Jesus, the King of kings, of course—and the Bible says he was a man after God's own heart (see Acts 13:22). But when God first chose David to do something great, he was nothing more than a scrawny kid who spent his days out in the field watching his family's sheep.

His father, Jesse, had seven strong, smart, handsome boys. They had bulging biceps. Sparkling white teeth. Perfect hair. None of them ever had a pimple. If Hollywood had issued a casting call for the next king of Israel, any one of them would have been perfect.

And then there was David.

God told the prophet Samuel to go to Jesse's house and anoint one of his sons as king. One by one, the strong, handsome brothers came before Samuel and turned on their charm. Every time, God said the same thing: "Nope. Not this one."

Seven times God said no. It left Samuel scratching his head in confusion.

"I don't get it," he told Jesse. "Do you have any more sons?"

"Well, there's David," Jesse replied, shaking his head. "But he can't be the one you're talking about. He's just a boy."

Samuel shrugged. "Well, bring him in. I need to see him."

You know the rest of the story. God revealed to Samuel that the shepherd boy was, indeed, the one God had chosen to lead His people. Samuel anointed the nation's future king while his brothers stood by, seething in unbelief (see 1 Samuel 16:1–13).

Actually, that is not quite the rest of the story.

You may remember that long before he became king of Israel, David also killed a warrior giant named Goliath. Goliath was a champion of the Philistines, a people at war with the Israelites. Every day, Goliath appeared before the Israelite camp and challenged someone to come out and meet him in battle. His offer was simple: "If one of you can defeat me, the Philistines will surrender and become your slaves. But if I prevail, then you must surrender and become our slaves" (see 1 Samuel 17:8–9).

Day after day, Goliath made the same challenge. And day after day—for forty days—the Israelites sat quaking in their tents, trying not to look each other in the eye because the wrong look might be misinterpreted as a desire to fight.

And who can blame them? Goliath was roughly the size of a Mack truck. (I realize they did not know what a Mack truck was back then, but hopefully that gives you an idea of how big this guy was.) Here's how Scripture describes this giant:

> His height was six cubits and a span. He had a bronze helmet on his head and wore a coat of scale armor of bronze weighing five thousand shekels; on his legs he wore bronze greaves, and a bronze javelin was slung on his back. His spear shaft was a like a weaver's rad, and its iron point weighed six hundred shekels.
>
> 1 Samuel 17:4–7

To give you an idea of what we are talking about here, first consider that this giant was more than nine feet tall. Then consider that it took about forty shekels to make a pound. Some simple calculations tell us the giant's coat of armor weighed 125 pounds and that the iron point of his spear weighed fifteen pounds. We are talking about Arnold Schwarzenegger on serious steroids here!

Goliath was a tower of a man. His arms looked like hams. When people said he had his head in the clouds, they did not mean he was always daydreaming. That is just how tall he was. His muscles had muscles. You would have to be a fool to take on somebody like him.

Or else you would have to have a lot of faith—like David.

You see, David knew who he was in God. He did not have to be afraid of this Philistine warrior because he embraced his true identity. He understood that "God plus one" is always an unbeatable combination.

Things came to a head when Jesse sent David to the front line with some care packages for his brothers who were serving in the Israelite army. While David was there, the giant issued his daily challenge. As usual, when the Israelites saw Goliath, they quaked in fear and ran (see 1 Samuel 17:24).

But David was not intimidated. Instead, he was offended none of God's people would take the bully's challenge. He asked the soldiers, "What will be done for the man who kills this Philistine and removes this disgrace from Israel?" (verse 26). I have heard some say David wanted to know how much money he would get, but I believe he was wondering if this was going to be the fulfillment of the anointing he had received from Samuel.

David's brothers acted in typical fashion when they heard their brother mouth off. They were ticked:

> When Eliab, David's oldest brother, heard him speaking with the men, he burned with anger at him and asked, "Why have you come down here? And with whom did you leave those few sheep in the wilderness? I know how conceited you are and how wicked your heart is; you came down only to watch the battle."
>
> 1 Samuel 17:28

Question: Were you aware David had a brother named Eliab? His is not exactly a household name, but he and

David came from the same family. They had the same genetic makeup. What made them so different? David understood his spiritual identity, but Eliab and David's other brothers did not—and so they became nothing more than footnotes in history.

Eliab was saying to David, "Who do you think you are, punk?" Remember, David was anointed king before his entire family. Eliab, as the eldest, would have been deeply insulted by this. Notice how he saw David's confidence and righteous anger as pride and conceit. The Identity Thief was in full swing here. David, stepping into his true identity, would be a serious threat to the kingdom of darkness.

I love David's response: "What have I done now? Is there not a cause?" (verse 29 NKJV). David was pleading for his brother to see past their personal differences. They were in a vitally important situation, one in which the entire nation was at risk.

Then we see that David "walked over to some others and asked them the same thing and received the same answer" (verse 30 NLT).

Poor David. Everyone was calling him out. No one could see past him being a prideful boy. Isn't it interesting, though, that they accused him of being prideful when it seems clear *their* pride was hurt. They were afraid to fight the giant, and so they were angry that this kid who was much too young to be in the army was willing to do it. They hated the fact that he had more courage and faith than they did!

Shortly thereafter, we find David going out to meet Goliath on the field of battle, saying to him:

> "You come against me with sword and spear and javelin, but I come against you in the name of the LORD Almighty, the God of the armies of Israel, whom you have defied. This

day the LORD will deliver you into my hands, and I'll strike you down and cut off your head. This very day . . . the whole world will know that there is a God in Israel. All those gathered here will know that it is not by sword or spear that the LORD saves; for the battle is the LORD's and he will give all of you into our hands."

1 Samuel 17:45–47

Not a bad speech for a punk kid going out to fight a guy more than nine feet tall! But these were not idle words. Remember what we said before: Faith is spelled R-I-S-K, and David cranked up the risk here. The Bible does not say the Lord showed David in a dream or through a word that he would defeat the giant. David had no assurances. He had only his unwavering faith in God.

And God came through. In short order, Goliath and the Philistines were defeated. I can almost imagine that as soon as David killed Goliath and cut off his head, all the Israelite army, including Eliab, burst into self-congratulatory applause—"Hooray! We did it!"—even though it was David, not them, who killed the giant.

The lesson here is that there is no limit to the good things we can accomplish if we walk out our true identity in Christ. The only person who believed David could defeat Goliath was David—and the God who packed a punch behind that "punk kid" He had chosen to be king. It was not arrogance or pride, as Eliab believed, but rather confidence in what the Lord would do. As David told the giant, "The battle is the LORD's" (verse 47).

All this is to say, do not fret if people put you down or criticize you. Determine to be a God-pleaser rather than a man-pleaser, and He will use you to accomplish great things.

Believe God Can Use You

A long time ago, a pastor friend of mine told me about an amusing incident that happened when he invited people to come forward to receive prayer for healing at the conclusion of a Sunday morning worship service.

An elderly man inched to the altar. After listening to the man's long list of serious ailments, my pastor friend said, "Okay, let's ask God to heal you."

The gentleman took a step back.

"No, I don't want you to pray for me to be healed," he said.

"You don't?"

"Oh, no. I just want you to pray that God will help me get a bus ticket to Tulsa, Oklahoma, so I can get Oral Roberts to pray for me. If I can do that, I know I'll be healed."

As you can see, this older gentleman had little confidence in his local pastor. The pastor might be good enough to pray for a Greyhound bus ticket, but when it came to healing, forget it.

I think a lot of Christians have that same attitude, especially in this age of celebrity worship. We see the superstars of the faith on television, and we think they are the only ones who can move the hand of God to give healing and perform miracles.

It is not true.

Now, please understand that I am not being critical of the men and women who preach the Gospel on television, write bestselling books or have become household names because they built megaministries. Thank God for them! They are touching millions of hearts and lives for Jesus every week.

At the same time, they do not have any special power or privilege that you do not also have as a follower of Jesus, such as watching miracles happen, praying for people and seeing them healed, and enabling the lame to get up and walk. These are all part of your spiritual identity as a disciple of Christ. We just need to live the R-I-S-K!

You and I are part of a priesthood believers. I cannot stress too strongly that God expects us to pray for one another, minister healing to the sick, bless those among us who are struggling financially and generally support each other in every way possible. Here's how the apostle Paul put it in his letter to the Ephesians:

> Christ himself gave the apostles, the prophets, the evangelists, the pastors and teachers, to equip his people for works of service, so that the body of Christ may be built up until we *all* reach unity in the faith and in the knowledge of the Son of God and become mature, attaining to the whole measure of the fullness of Christ.
> . . . From him *the whole body*, joined and held together by every supporting ligament, grows and builds itself up in love, as each part does its work.
>
> Ephesians 4:11–13, 16, emphasis added

I added emphasis to the words *all* and *the whole body* above because I want to draw attention to Paul's reference to Body ministry. Every member of the Body is important, and every member has a vital role to play. My role is important, and so is yours. We must not forget that. Remember that vision of ordinary people healing other ordinary people in my dream?

Perhaps you have had the difficult experience of praying fervently for someone and not seeing an immediate answer. If this is the case, please do not give up! Keep on knocking, seeking and asking, and God will begin to respond.

Along those lines, you might want to take a look at John Wimber's classic book *Power Healing*.[1] For ten months after

Wimber and his congregation came to the realization they should be praying for the sick, nothing happened. It seemed not a single prayer was answered. Wimber wrote honestly in his book about his agony and despair over the lack of results.

Finally, after that long, dry spell, the healings and miracles began to come. When it happened, Wimber received a vision of a giant honeycomb in the sky, dripping honey on the people below. Some were weeping and holding their hands out to catch it, while others acted irritated and complained about the sticky mess.

Wimber acknowledged his experience was not typical. He knew many Christians who saw God respond in amazing ways the first time they prayed for healing. I have seen the same. Remember my story about the young man who prayed for the deaf man's hearing to be restored? But if you have begun to doubt your prayers are effective, please keep on seeking God, and you will see His mercy fall like honey.

Know that it is never God's objective for you to fail. He wants you to prosper and reign with Him. And if God is with you, who can possibly be against you? Nobody!

10

RECEIVE A NEW HEART

"I will give you a new heart and put a new spirit in you; I
will remove from you your heart of stone and give you a
heart of flesh."

Ezekiel 36:26

Shortly after God gave me that amazing dream and the
prophecy through Dan White, I met a pastor at a conference
who told me he was looking for a youth pastor. His church
had a great tradition. Billy Graham had preached there. So
had Oral Roberts. But after the founding pastor died, the
church fell upon hard times.

This pastor and his wife were wonderful people—two of
the finest people of God I have ever met. The church itself
was a bit old-fashioned. It was one of those churches where
the choir members all wore robes and sat in the choir loft
every Sunday. Only two teenagers attended regularly, and yet

the church hired me as youth pastor at twice the salary I had been making before. They really needed a strong evangelist, someone who could go into the community and bring young people to Christ and into the church.

So, we got a group together to refurbish the old, rundown youth room, and we started holding meetings there. Within a few months, we started averaging 25 kids, but I wanted to do more to reach young people for Christ.

That is when God gave me the idea of holding a youth conference and inviting kids from the city. I lined up some well-known speakers and musicians who were friends of mine, invited a great band from another church in town and started putting up posters around town. The conference, which we called Impact Weekend, turned out to be a terrific success. About five hundred teenagers attended. We shared great times of worship, the guy who did the preaching knocked it out of the park and many teens were saved.

Rocked by God

It was while I was at that church that I first heard the name John Wimber, founder of the group known as the Association of Vineyard Churches. The story is told in more detail in my first book, *Do What Jesus Did*, but because it was such an important event in my life, I want to briefly retell it here.

At this time, I was skeptical of anything that smacked of what I considered charismatic excess. Because of hurtful experiences in my past, I was extremely cautious—and even a bit cynical.

One Sunday night, a woman from Finland came to speak at the church. As I listened, I thought whoever had invited her had made a big mistake. Her English was so poor that I

Receive a New Heart

found it difficult to keep track of what she was saying. One thing I did understand—at least a little—was that she had gone through a lot of struggles in her life until she went to a meeting where John Wimber was preaching. (She called him Vimber.) She talked about "getting drunk" at that meeting and then going out to pray for people.

It did not make much sense to me. I should have known she was talking about being drunk in the Spirit (see Ephesians 5:18). But my heart was closed to her, and I suppose I did not really want to understand.

It only got worse when she finished her talk and asked people to come forward for prayer. Everyone she prayed for fell over backward, and I did not like it. I knew that "falling out under the Spirit" or "being slain in the Spirit" was a real manifestation of God's presence. I had seen it before, beginning in middle school when that guest speaker prayed for me to receive the Holy Spirit. But I was convinced it had become a fad among charismatic Christians and that what was going on in many churches was not real. I had even seen people look over their shoulder to make sure someone was there to catch them when they fell to the floor. I had also seen some evangelists push people hard to get them to fall over.

Angie and I had been prayed for a number of times by people who wanted us to fall over, but it never happened. This was more proof to me that it was not real.

Back to the story. I was so upset by what was going on in the service that I wanted to leave, even though I was the youth pastor. Angie had other ideas.

"I'm going up for prayer!" she said.

"You're crazy!" I replied.

She did not listen. Imagine my surprise when she fell to the floor, just like the others had done.

165

I finally decided I would go up for prayer, too. But I decided I was not going to fall down. I hate to say it now, because I know I was wrong, but my real intention in going forward for prayer was to show that the woman speaker was a fraud.

Now, I am a big guy. When I got up there, I braced myself like a football lineman waiting for the opposing player to crash into him. There was absolutely no way this little lady was going to get me to fall over unless the Holy Spirit was involved.

She reached up to touch my head—but then she seemed to change her mind.

"No," she said. "Fadder, You do it."

As she said that, I started tipping backward in the air. I was shocked. I saw the ceiling spin past my eyes, and I hollered, "No way!" Just as I said the word *way*, I froze in that position—mouth open, eyes wide in disbelief, hands frozen by my head like claws, in shock. The guy catching people did not catch me until I was eighteen inches from the ground. The impact of my weight split his pants from zipper to belt loop. He had to borrow a woman's sweater to tie around his waist for the rest of the evening.

I stayed on the ground, frozen, for about three hours, tears streaming out of my eyes. I knew something was happening to me, but I did not know what. I did not feel anything in particular, but I was frozen in place. I remember my eyes were open the whole time, and I was thinking, *Why am I crying? Why am I crying?*

As I lay on the floor, I had a vision of dry bones, very much like the vision of dry bones described by the prophet Ezekiel (see Ezekiel 37:1–14). Brittle, decaying bones were spread out before me. Wherever I looked, I saw nothing but parched bones baking in the sun.

God spoke to me and told me to prophesy to those bones, so I did. Where nothing but a desolate boneyard had been, thousands and thousands of strong, healthy people came together, ready to march forward to advance God's Kingdom. I knew this was His Church.

Then the Lord spoke to me again and said, *That's what I am calling you to do. But never forget you were the most dry pile of bones.*

That was a pivotal moment in my life as a Christ-follower and in my work as a pastor and evangelist. I began to hear God's voice more clearly. When I prayed for people who were not Christian, they had a strong sense of God's presence. As I said in *Do What Jesus Did*, "They suddenly knew He was real, and they responded. I had never seen anything like that before, but for me, it was the beginning of a journey toward understanding what it means to be a carrier of His presence."[1]

Here Comes Trouble

God was at work. And Satan was angry. Trouble was on the way.

The first thing I knew, I started hearing complaints that the main speaker I had invited to do one of our Impact Weekends was black. This shocked and saddened me because he was a powerful man of God. I hated that people would judge him simply because of the color of his skin.

After that, there were complaints about some of the young people who came into the church. Our youth program was booming, but people did not like the fact that some of the kids came from wild backgrounds. They did not like the fact that these young people had tattoos. They did not like the way these kids dressed. It did not matter that these youth had put their hedonistic lifestyles behind them and come to

Christ. Some people did not want them around because they were not clean-cut, all-American kids. After all, this was a church where nearly everyone wore suits to all the services.

People were also upset the pastor wanted to move the church into a more contemporary style of worship. They saw it as a threat to their identity. "But we've always done it this way," they protested.

The congregation wound up calling for a vote of affirmation for the pastor. I was confident he would be supported by an overwhelming majority. I was wrong. This godly, righteous man lost by one vote and was dismissed from the church that very day.

The church board asked me to stay on and even offered me the pastor's position, but I would not take it. I knew the same thing could happen to me. I was told I was free to take the church in any direction I saw fit, but I figured they said that because I was young and they thought I would do anything they wanted me to do. I tried to stay there and fight for what was right, but it did not work.

After a couple months, two of the elders came and asked me to resign. What they did not know was that I had already ordered a moving truck. God had already opened another door, and Angie and I were on our way to Illinois.

A Mennonite Miracle

What happened was that I had called a friend of mine at Christ for the Nations and asked if he knew of anyone looking for a youth pastor.

"Yes, I've got the perfect place for you," he said. "You'll be perfect for them. I'll give you the phone number, but I'm not going to give you the name of the church."

"Why not?"

"Don't ask. Just call them."

When I did, the secretary answered, "Brethren Mennonite Church."

When the pastor came on the phone, I said, "I'm sorry, but can you tell me the name of this church again?"

He chuckled and said, "Brethren Mennonite Church."

"Mennonite?" I asked.

"Are you calling about the youth pastor position?"

"Yes, but I don't know anything about the Mennonites. Are you the ones who still use horses and buggies?"

He laughed. "You're thinking of the Amish."

He went on to explain the origin of the Mennonites and said that Brethren Mennonite was a Spirit-filled Mennonite church. He asked if I would have any trouble with that.

I said, "No, not as long as I can drive my car and don't have to dress in black and blue all the time."

The church was in a small bedroom community in Illinois that had around six thousand residents. Angie and I had always lived in the city, but we loved this beautiful small town. We loved the people, too. There were maybe two hundred fifty people in the church, and they all seemed to love each other.

Now, I had not been there long when a few of the people went up to Toronto to attend services at the Vineyard Fellowship. A powerful revival was under way, and they wanted to see firsthand what was going on there.

The next Sunday, I was in for a surprise as I walked into the church office prior to my Sunday school class. One of the church staff—a proper Mennonite lady named Norma—was laughing and waving her hands around in the air like she was drunk. As I walked by, she blew on me and said, "You need to receive what I've got."

I thought, *Man, she's lost her mind.*

I walked into the pastor's office to see if he knew what was going on. Now, this was a man who was always impeccably dressed. Every hair was always in place. The knot in his tie was perfectly straight as a rule—but today it was cocked off to the side.

"Pastor," I asked, "have you seen Norma?"

"Why? What's wrong?"

"She's laughing like a crazy woman."

He stood up, slapped his leg and started guffawing. "Oh, Robby, you have no idea! We just went to the most amazing thing in Toronto. This is going to change our church."

I thought, *Yeah, it's going to change us into a nuthouse.* I edged closer to see if he had been drinking.

In the service that day, all the people who had been to Toronto kept laughing and slapping their legs, and I did not like it one bit. I turned to Angie and said, "This isn't right. I'm going to put an end to it."

I stepped up to the open microphone, and the worship leader said, "I think Robby has a word for us."

To my great surprise, I heard myself say, "I have a word from the Lord. I hear the Lord saying, 'This is it. Get in.'"

I walked back to my seat, and Angie asked, "Why did you say that?"

I shook my head. "I don't know. All I know is that was weird. I don't know why or how that happened."

Hands in the Air

The following week, Jean Chapman, the church secretary who had also been to Toronto, brought me a video she wanted me to watch.

I was not sure I wanted to watch it. "This is kind of weird to me," I said.

She insisted I needed to watch it, so I agreed I would. I rolled a VCR and monitor into my office—this being 1994—and put in the video. As it turned out, I enjoyed the worship and the teaching by Larry Randolph, a great preacher with a terrific sense of humor. When he got to the end of his talk, he invited the ministry team to come up.

One of the women on the team was obviously disabled. Her head and her arms were shaking, and I thought, *That's so good of them to put this woman with Parkinson's on the ministry team.* Almost immediately, though, both of her arms shot straight up into the air. *Wait a minute*, I realized. *She's not disabled.* Every few minutes, her hands shot up into the air, and I did not like it.

"That's not God!" I yelled.

The very next time her hands shot up into the air, though, mine did the same thing. I thought, *Oh, my, what is that?*

After that, every time her hands went up, mine did the same. I still did not like it, so I got up and turned off the monitor. Even so, my arms kept shooting into the air every minute or two. I looked at the VCR and saw the numbers still moving in the little window. I had turned off the monitor, but the video was still playing. When I turned the video off, the "craziness" stopped.

When I told Jean later that I did not care much for the video, she asked, "Did you like the worship?"

"Yes."

"Did you like the teaching?"

"Well, yeah."

"You need to watch another video," she said, "and this time watch it all the way through."

I agreed, and the next video she gave me featured Randy Clark giving his testimony. I was touched by his genuineness and his humility. I had never heard a pastor be as open and vulnerable as he was. I remember thinking, *This is a man I could follow*. I could feel the presence of God as he spoke, so I knew an anointing was on him.

Heart on the Floor

During that time, I felt something of a disconnect with what was going on for some at the church. I desired a deeper, stronger relationship with God, but I was skeptical of the "holy laughter" and other experiences that had come to us via the Toronto Vineyard.

I was reading a book by Winkie Pratney called *Revival: Its Principles and Personalities*, and it was making an impact on me. I was stirred when I read about the Cane Ridge Revival and also about Charles Finney's conversion. He described experiencing waves of what he called *liquid love*. Sometimes he could not tell if he had been in his office three hours or three days as wave after wave of divine love washed over him. As I read, I thought, *I don't know the God of Charles Finney. I don't know what he has experienced. I want to know God in that way.*

I was thinking about this one day when Jean walked into my office with some letters for me to sign. She stopped and said, "Did you hear what I just said to you? God is in your office right now."

I said, "All I know is that I'm sick and tired of being a wimpy, man-pleasing leader in the Body of Christ."

As soon as the words were out of my mouth, I began to feel something deep in the pit of my stomach. It felt like nausea, and it was rising up in my throat. I feared I was going to puke all over my office. When I opened my mouth to let it out, I began laughing like a madman.

I could not stop laughing. I was laughing and laughing and laughing. Jean told me later, "Your eyes showed sheer terror, but your mouth was experiencing a party." I felt some type of purging taking place.

The phone rang, so Jean stepped out of my office.

Suddenly, my chair flew into the air with me in it and dumped me onto the floor. The chair went one way and I went another. It lifted so fast off the floor that all the casters popped out. I lay on the floor facedown, laughing and laughing.

As I lay there, the Lord spoke to me and said, *I'm going to give you a brand-new heart.* I felt immense pain and pressure in my chest, like I was having a heart attack, and I began to convulse. My head was banging against the carpet-covered cement floor.

Jean, hearing the noise, tried to come over to make sure I was okay, but the presence of God was so strong she could not stand up. Instead, she had to get down and crawl over to me, military style, bringing me a pillow from the couch to place under my head to soften the blows.

Seven times over the next four hours, I felt the sensation of a hand reaching through my back and grabbing my heart, and each time I thought I would die right there.

Toward the end of this incredible experience, I had a stirring vision. I saw myself climbing a hill in the dark without a flashlight. When I got to the top of the hill, I saw Jesus, and it was like that famous painting where the Lord is looking over Jerusalem and saying, "Jerusalem, Jerusalem, you who kill the prophets and stone those sent to you, how often I have longed to gather your children together, as a hen gathers her chicks under her wings, and you were not willing" (Matthew 23:37).

Then it was not ancient Jerusalem but a modern city, full of electricity and cars and light. As Jesus looked out, He said, *Oh, My church, My church. You're so full of power, and yet I'm not the source of that power. You've learned to manufacture your own power.*

I began to weep. I am not sure I even understood it, but I began to wail. I had this immense feeling of loss, grief and sadness as I heard Jesus weep over His people.

In the vision, I heard a noise and looked to the left. Coming up the back of the hill was a disheveled group of people making their way through the dark. They had no flashlights. They looked ragged and lost. Jesus turned their way and opened His arms to receive them . . . and then it was over.

When I got off the floor, there was a puddle under my head of all the sweat, snot and tears I had cried. I ran to the restroom and looked in the mirror and did not recognize myself. I literally reached out to touch the mirror in shock.

When I got home that afternoon, Angie met me at the door. When she saw me, she turned her head to the side and asked, "What happened to you?"

"What do you mean?"

"You look different."

"What do you mean?"

"You look totally different. And you sound different. Something's happened."

Before I could explain, my mom called on the phone.

I picked it up and said, "Hello?"

"Oh, hi, this is Robby's mom," she said.

"I know who you are. You would not believe what happened to me today. Something so strange happened that I can't even put it into words."

"Well, I'd love to hear about that sometime," she said, "but I called to talk to my son."

"Mom, it's me!"

It was like she didn't hear me. "Well, let me talk to Robby."

"Mom! It's Robby!"

"Really?"

I could tell she was surprised.

"You don't sound like yourself at all," she said.

God had changed me. My life would never be the same after that.

11

I GOT TORONTOED

For the kingdom of God is not in word but in power.

1 Corinthians 4:20 NKJV

After my amazing encounter with God in my office, evangelism went to an entirely new level for me. There was a power in my words that attracted people when I spoke. They seemed anxious to hear about Jesus and ready to respond to His invitation to come to God through Him. And now that I had experienced His love and power in such an incredible way, I was more anxious than ever before to tell everyone about Him.

I had been skeptical of what I had heard about what was going on at the Toronto Vineyard, but it is difficult to doubt what you have experienced for yourself. When an opportunity arose for me to travel to Toronto and take part in the revival there, I was all for it. What an incredible experience it was!

As a group of us from Illinois were making our way into the building, a man came up and asked, "Where's the sanctuary?"

I pointed. "Just keep going."

As he continued, he began to crouch over and waddle. Yes, waddle. Like a duck. I called out to him and asked him if he had been to this gathering before.

"No, this is my first time," he responded.

Clearly, he was walking directly into the power and presence of God.

We felt it, too, as soon as we walked inside. There was a roar in the room as people ministered to each other, received healing and fell under the power of the Holy Spirit. It was exactly what I had seen in that Moses dream all those years ago.

A Drunken Moment

As we made our way to our seats, some ushers handed us sheets of paper so we could write out and turn in our testimonies. By doing this, we were agreeing to come up front and share our testimonies from the pulpit if they called our names.

I turned to Angie and told her I was going to write an account of what had happened in my office. Her eyes told me she did not want me to do it. She was afraid I would be disappointed if I did not get called.

"There are thousands of people here," she said. "What are the chances they're going to pick your testimony?"

"We'll see," I said, as I began to write out the story.

Toward the end of the worship, I looked at a vent in the ceiling and saw something like water starting to drip out of it. It looked sort of airy, like a mirage. Whatever it was, it kept getting closer. Finally, it fell, landing on the bridge of my nose, where it started to dance around. When this happened, I felt a light, tickly, giddy feeling inside and started laughing. It felt like the same effect laughing gas has on you at the dentist.

Wouldn't you know it, the whole place had grown quiet as people worshiped God, so Angie nudged me.

"What are you doing?" she asked.

I turned to her with a big smile on my face and said, "They're about to call my name."

As soon as the words were out of my mouth, one of the leaders stepped to the microphone and said, "We're going to do testimonies. Is Robby Dawkins here?"

I smiled at Angie. "See? I told you!"

I started walking to the front. Now, I have seen a video tape from the occasion, and from the tape, I can see that I began moving in slow motion as I walked. I thought I was walking normally at the time, but when I watch the video, it looks like I am walking on the moon.

When I got on stage, I felt unsteady on my feet. *I think I'm drunk*, I thought, making Ephesians 5:18 take on new significance: "And be not drunk with wine, wherein is excess; but be filled with the Spirit" (KJV).

Someone was talking to me.

"Now, listen, you wrote your testimony," they whispered. "Can you please share your story—and stick to what you wrote on the paper?"

I was confused. "Paper? What paper? I wrote a paper?"

I was not sure what the person was talking about, but I launched in.

"You know," I said, "I'm sitting back here, and all of a sudden this stuff started falling from the vent up there. Then it began dancing on the bridge of my nose. And I started to feel this fluttery feeling. And now I feel this great joy and this love."

"Stick to the story," the man whispered to me again.

Oh, that's right. My testimony. I remembered now.

I managed to talk about what happened in my office, but I told it really slow, and my speech became more slurred as I went along. When watching the video later, I realized I left out quite a bit of the story. And when I got to the end, I said, "All I know is that what's happening in this room right now is God, and this is it. This is really it." I didn't realize it at the time, but those were very nearly the same words I had used back home when I had tried to speak against the move of God in the church service.

John Arnott, pastor of the Toronto Vineyard, was standing to my left. He turned to me and said, "Bless you, Robby." Three simple words. But when he said them, it was like a strong blast of air hit me in the chest, and I just went down—*bam!*—and hit the floor.

When I watched the video later, I could see that my legs kept flying into the air, first one, then the other, like I was riding a bicycle. When another man came up to share his testimony, he, too, hit the floor. I started rocking back and forth, moving from side to side, and he was doing the same thing. The two of us looked like we were synchronized swimmers. We stayed there on the floor for the duration of the service, rocking back and forth, drunk with the Spirit.

I told someone later that if we could take this power and bottle it, it could change the world. I did not know anything about the Vineyard movement at the time, nor did I know anything about power evangelism, but I thought, *If this is the Vineyard, I want in.*

A Familiar Refrain

When I got back to my church, I was determined to reach the town's youth for Christ. One of the first things we did was start taking hotdogs to the kids at the "smokers' corner" at the high school. This was where the students who smoked gathered to spend their lunchtime, and I figured they spent whatever money they had on cigarettes instead of food. Some of them were rough characters, but I knew they needed Jesus. So we gave them hotdogs and drinks, and I would play Hacky Sack with them. Then I would tell them about Jesus and invite them to our youth group.

Many of them came. Our youth room would be packed out, but a lot of the kids would stand outside and smoke before and after the service, and some of the church members did not like it.

After a few weeks of this, the pastor came to me and said, "The kids you're attracting—they're not the sort of youth we want. I want you to come up with a plan to help us attract upper-middle-class kids into the youth group."

Where had I seen this type of thinking before? Oh, that's right—at my last church.

I knew that many, or even most, of these young people had been fooled into believing what the devil told them about themselves. He told them they were troublemakers, outsiders, unwanted. And now I was hearing the church and my pastor tell them that, too. I knew God wanted to show them who they really were: precious people created in His own image. But it seemed many within the church had also fallen for Satan's lie.

A few days later, a group of us gathered at the church to discuss our evangelism strategies. In the course of our conversation, I said, "Man, if we could experience what they were doing in Toronto, we'd bring everybody to Jesus."

The pastor sat there in stony silence. What I did not know was that, even though he had once been extremely enthusiastic about what had taken place in Toronto, he had moved away from it because he was getting some pressure from those in the congregation who thought it was weird.

A Rancorous Division

Sunday morning, April 30, 1995, I was moderating a service when I felt the presence of God building in the room. The tingling in my chest and down my arms let me know God was there in a special way.

The church had a rule that any time one of the pastors or elders sensed the Lord wanted to take the service in a different direction, he or she had to share it with the other elders first. They would only allow it if they felt an assurance from God it was genuine.

So, while the congregation was worshiping, I got the elders together and said, "Hey, I think we need to let the Spirit rip in this place. I feel like the balloon is about to pop."

The elders agreed, but the senior pastor never said a word either way. According to my understanding, the decision did not have to be unanimous.

I stepped up to the microphone and said, "The Holy Spirit is here, and He's about to fall on this room. It's about to erupt in fire. Put your hands out. Holy Spirit, come!"

About a third of the congregation erupted into laughter, including all of the worship team. Some started weeping. Others fell over. I asked if anyone wanted to come forward for prayer, and about half the congregation did.

About a third of the folks sat in their chairs with their arms crossed and angry looks on their faces. They did not like it at all.

On Monday, the pastor called me into his office and told me, "We didn't have a full confirmation on the direction you took the service."

I tried to explain. "Well, the other three elders all agreed that it was what we should do, and our policy has always been that the majority vote rules."

He shook his head. "But I didn't agree. I didn't like it, and I don't want you to do it again."

I was incredulous. "But I've only experienced this because of you," I said. "You're the one who brought this to the church."

"I don't want you to do it again," he repeated.

I knew immediately the Identity Thief was at work. Satan was trying to steal the church's identity. From its inception, the church had been known as a charismatic Mennonite Church—a place where the Holy Spirit and His gifts were welcome. But now, instead of moving deeper into the things of the Spirit, it seemed we were turning away from our heritage.

After that, things became increasingly tense between the pastor and me. It seemed he found fault with everything I did, and I was constantly feeling stressed and under pressure. Again, I know now it was all due to the attack of the Identity Thief.

One night I had a dream where I was walking through the halls of the church, and I heard footsteps behind me. When I looked back, I saw the pastor following me with an intense look on his face. I picked up my pace, and so did he. Clearly, he was chasing me.

Then the walls of the church turned to stone, and we were in a dimly lit cave. I was now wearing clothes more suited to Old Testament times. I again looked back and saw the pastor was now dressed in full armor, with a javelin in one

IDENTITY **THIEF**

hand and a sword in the other. I felt like David running from the anger of King Saul.

I woke up in a sweat, my heart racing, and knew I had received a warning from the Lord.

After that, things got worse, and fast. The pastor who had founded the congregation was brought in to discuss the situation with us. He took me aside and confirmed the current pastor felt God telling him to take the church in a different direction—and because of this, it was best for me to leave. He advised me what to do, and I followed his advice.

A Call to Freedom

Around this time, I got a call from a friend of mine named Tom Morrison. Tom was a prophet ministering at a church in the Chicago area. He said, "I'm doing a conference with a man named Chuck Pierce this weekend. Chuck is a real prophet, and I feel like you should come up here and be a part of this. I think the Lord wants to speak to you here."

Of course, I was happy to go.

The first night of the conference, Chuck called me to the front of the congregation and said, "The Lord has something to say to Robby."

When I went forward, he told me, "You have the heart of an evangelist in you. The enemy has been trying to take your ministry away, but you are called to powerful evangelism—and you are going to equip many people for powerful evangelism. The enemy is threatened by that, so he's trying to cause strife and tension. But listen to me. The day is going to come when you're going to preach and thousands at a time will come to Christ. Even tens of thousands. You're going

184

to preach and people will be stirred. You're going to raise up thousands and even tens of thousands who will bring millions to Christ."

He went on, "The enemy has tried to come after you, and you've been afraid of something. But I want you to know the Lord is going to have you overturn the altar even of your father—the altar that your father sacrificed on that is not the altar of God. You're going to overturn it, and you're going to defeat it."

That word hit me so hard. The Holy Spirit was telling me I was free, that I didn't have to follow in the footsteps of my father—footsteps that led into sexual sin. Looking back on the day my dad told me what he had done, I remember almost feeling like he was confessing he was really a pagan. It was like he did not really believe any of the things he had been preaching all those years. What a relief it was to know now I was totally free from that legacy. Tears streamed down my face as that fear was lifted from my shoulders.

Then Tom, who was standing there with us, broke in.

"Let me say something," he said. "You've been telling God, 'I'll do anything for You. But there's one thing I won't do.' That's what I want you to do. Just so you know, I'm going to bless you in it. At the time when the wind blows the leaves off the trees, I'm going to blow you to another place, where you'll do that thing that you've said, 'God, I'll do anything, but I won't do this.'"

I knew immediately what it was. I had always said I would never plant churches. My grandfather did that, and so did my father. It is extremely hard work, and you can practically starve to death while you are doing it. No, I had always thought, *that is not the life for me.*

Apparently, the Lord thought otherwise.

Tom continued, "I have placed the cry of freedom inside of you. I will take you around the world, and you will cry the cry of freedom, and young people will follow you by the thousands into the freedom, and then they will continue the cry."

(I should pause here and say this happened a month before the movie *Braveheart* was released—a fitting parallel to this prophetic word from Tom.)

Even so, despite the indication that God was inviting me to plant churches, when I got back to my home church, I figured I had better make some calls to find out if any churches were in need of a pastor. After all, God did not say I needed to get busy planting churches right away.

After what I had experienced in Toronto, I felt sure the Vineyard was the way for me to go. It turned out there were two Vineyard churches in our area looking for pastors. Angie and I visited them both. The first one seemed to be a wonderful church, but almost as soon as we walked through the door, we both felt the Lord saying, "No, this is not the church for you." So we left before the interview took place.

I went to the second place and spoke there, but it turned out the elders of the congregation felt I was "too strong" of a leader. However, the man who oversaw the Vineyard churches in the area felt I was the man for the job. He called the church's elders and read them the riot act. He told them he believed they had made a bad decision, that a strong leader was exactly what they needed and that John Wimber never would have approved of the decision they had made.

The very next Sunday, one of the elders stood up in front of the congregation and asked, "How many of you are here this morning because this is a Vineyard church? Will you please stand up?"

Ten or twelve people stood up.

The elder pointed at the door. "Well, there's the door. You can leave right now, because this is no longer a Vineyard."

Once again, the Identity Thief was at work in a dramatic way.

Immediately after this happened, one of the expelled couples from the church called us and said, "Hey, why don't you come plant a church with us?"

I remembered what God had said to me through Tom Morrison, but I did not know if this was the right move. Would it be a good idea to start a church with a bunch of people who had been mistreated and were probably hurt and angry? What did God want me to do?

That is the story we will turn to next.

12

GOD WORKS IN THE THIEF'S LAIR

"For I know the plans I have for you," declares the LORD, "plans to prosper you and not to harm you, plans to give you hope and a future."

Jeremiah 29:11

I have to admit I still resisted the idea of becoming a church planter. But it also seemed clear God was leading me in that direction. The prophecy from Tom Morrison was clear. After hearing his words, I knew better than to think what had happened at the little Vineyard church was a coincidence. Clearly, God was at work. Not that I believe God was responsible for the church split. Satan loves it when Christians fight each other and churches split, so I know he was behind it. But God knows how to bring good out of what the devil plans for bad. As usual, Satan played directly into God's hands.

With all that in mind, Angie and I decided that, yes, we would drive up and meet with the folks who wanted us to help them start a new church, and we would see where that led us. We planned to meet them in a suburb of Chicago, about 45 minutes past the city of Aurora.

A City Loved by Jesus

Somehow, I managed take a wrong turn on our way to the meeting, though, and we wound up in Aurora. Now, I am pretty good at finding my way around. I travel all over the world, and I am not the type to take wrong turns and get lost. But as the Bible says, "In their hearts humans plan their course, but the LORD establishes their steps" (Proverbs 16:9).

Angie and I both knew the Holy Spirit had caused us to take that wrong turn. We both had an impression Aurora was where God wanted us to be. But it certainly was not because we were attracted by the city's beauty. Aurora is a city of about two hundred thousand people, and it has some beautiful architecture and some neighborhoods with lovely homes and well-manicured lawns.

But we did not see any of that. Instead, we wound up in the worst, most rundown part of the city—and it was bad. I am talking about the sort of place where you lock your car doors while you are driving through because you do not want anyone to try to carjack you while you are stopped at a red light.

We drove past block after block of dilapidated or shuttered businesses. Ragged homeless people wandered past, pushing shopping carts filled with all their worldly belongings. Others sat on sidewalks, slumped against vacant buildings, staring out as the world passed them by. And some staggered aimlessly down the city's streets, obviously strung out on drugs. Some of the homes and businesses we passed had bars on the windows for protection.

This was no garden spot. It was not the sort of area where parents would want their children to grow up. But we were seeing it with the eyes of Jesus, who wanted so desperately to let these lost people know how much He loves them. Jesus was the only way out of the pain, poverty and addiction that gripped them, and it seemed to both Angie and me that this was where He wanted us to plant a church. I recalled the words of the great missionary C. T. Studd: "Some wish to live within the sound of a chapel bell; I wish to run a rescue mission within a yard of hell."

It took about fifteen minutes or so to get back on the correct route and resume our trip. We were quiet at first because we were sobered by what we had seen, and we were also excited and a bit apprehensive about what God was saying to us. As we began to talk about it, our excitement only grew while our apprehension began to melt away. I was thrilled to know the Holy Spirit was saying the same thing to both of us.

When we finally reached the correct destination and met with the group that wanted to start a new church, we were impressed. Without exception, these were people who loved God and wanted to serve Him.

We met with them for several months. Then one night we had a special planning meeting about our official start. One of the items up for discussion was where we would locate our new church.

"What do you think about Aurora?" I asked.

One of the men laughed and shook his head. "Oh, it's a terrible place," he said, and the others agreed. Nobody thought much of Aurora, it seemed.

"Well," I told them, "we both feel that is where God wants us to be."

Shortly after that conversation, most everyone pulled out of the plant. Angie and I were the only ones who wanted to go to Aurora. Some were quite angry we would even consider it. But we felt this was where God wanted us.

Over the next few weeks, a kind businessman rented us some space at an unbelievably low rate. After three months there, we moved to the border of the city. It was not the worst section, but it was close enough for us to start what turned out to be a seventeen-year stay of pastoring in Aurora, Illinois.

God Comes to Work

At the time, I desperately needed a job to feed my family. I still had all my carpet equipment and carpet-installation tools, but since I had not done that type of work in a while, I felt rather rusty. But Angie and I prayed about it, and I set out one afternoon looking for a job.

Through God's grace, I found one almost immediately. The owner of the store even waived his stipulation that any new hire had to have been working in the business the past five years. Within the next week, I had four installations. This was yet another sign God had us right where He wanted us to be. His blessing was evident.

During one of those jobs, I installed carpet for a woman who was afraid to leave her house. I sensed she had a spirit of fear, and I told her so. As soon as I did, she started manifesting. She fell to the freshly installed carpet and began to shake violently. I stopped what I was doing, rushed over to her and began to minister deliverance. It took about twenty minutes to get the demon to leave, but eventually the victory was won. The woman began to cry, sobbing, "It's gone. It's finally gone." She told me she had been tormented for five years, and now she knew she had been set free.

Our entire time in Aurora, we were learning to walk in the strength of our spiritual identity. From our first day there, we were engaged in a spiritual battle. Early on, we realized we had to move to an offensive position of warfare. We were not going to sit back and pray protection prayers while huddled in the corner. We had to take the fight to the enemy.

At the time, our first two sons were very small, and Angie was pregnant with child number three. I was a hands-on dad, so after laying carpet all day, I would still want to eat dinner as a family and put the boys to bed. Then I would take a team to the local bars and pray for people there.

What we found was amazing. Most people were willing to open up and share their troubles, and they were happy to have us pray for them.

As we did, God began to move in a mighty way. People were healed and delivered. They would show up at the church saying they had come because they had heard the presence of God was there.

One day, the manager of our building, a guy named Gary, was coming to fix a broken thermostat. He was screaming at me over the phone about the problem, which people told me was his usual attitude. But when he walked through the door, everything changed. He even ran over and hugged me. I thought I would swallow my tongue.

He told me, "Robby, I have been very angry for years, but as soon as I walked through that door, all of my rage just left me. I can't explain it. I just walked in, it left, and joy flooded me."

Gary wound up giving his life to Christ, as did his whole family. He discovered that anger and rage were not his true identity, and he became a gracious volunteer for our church.

In my carpet work, I started hiring people who were coming out of a violent past, including drug addiction and gang activity. I would use the carpet business to teach them a trade, then set them up with their own set of tools or carpet-cleaning machine, and they would spin off on their own. I would show them that their true identity was not that of a thug but of a true contributor to the community.

Other times I would be laying carpet when I would notice a twinge in my back. I would ask the customer if they had back trouble, and when they said yes, I would have my helper lay hands on the owner and command their body to be healed. We were living the naturally supernatural lifestyle, and the Identity Thief was losing his grip on our city.

When we were done for the day, my knuckles would be bloody, my knees would be aching, sweat would be pouring off me and my back would be hurting from the tension of the work. I would go out to my van, where I kept a copy of the prophecy Dan White gave me. I would start with, "Lord, You said . . . ," and read it again. I drew so much comfort from those words.

I was not bitter about having to work so hard as a church planter, small-business owner and father of a young family. I was just letting the Lord know I was not waiting for that word to be fulfilled. I saw it as an invitation to start where I was. I learned that changing the world starts across the street, in the cubical or at the locker next to you. That is how I started, and since then I have ministered in 46 different countries.

There were many difficult times in Aurora. More than once, our lives were threatened by gangsters who did not want us stirring up trouble by teaching people about Jesus. Our hearts were broken when those who were addicted to drugs and alcohol or were struggling to survive on the streets refused to take the hand of the One who wanted to lift them out of their need and poverty and restore their identity as His children. Our growing family cried many tears over the lives of those we discipled who were murdered.

They were difficult years, yes, but we also saw God at work.

Luci Pays the Price

My pet name for Satan is Little Luci—short for Lucifer. I always imagine him as a young lad, rosy cheeks, in a tutu with pigtails. (If you are offended by that image, that is okay, because so is he.)

One day, a couple named Dave and Steph showed up at church. They had really struggled with heroin and crack. Dave really wanted to get free, but Steph kept pulling him back into addiction. She just could not quit the pipe. We ended up finding a home for them. Things looked good at first, but then Steph started hooking to get money for drugs. We helped Dave get a job, and he was working hard, but Steph just could not get straight.

Steph's mother was practicing witchcraft and dabbled as a psychic reader. She called me one day, saying, "Steph is hooking, and it has to stop. The only way she'll quit drugs and hooking is to get arrested."

I said, "Okay, I'll pray about that, and she'll be arrested tomorrow. That will let you know Jesus loves you and wants a relationship with you."

The woman laughed. We had worked hard for Steph's record to be settled with the police, and there were no outstanding warrants. It seemed unlikely an arrest would happen, much less happen tomorrow.

The next morning, though, I got a call from Steph.

"I've been arrested, and I'm not sure why they're holding me," she said.

She was in custody for ten days and then agreed to go to a facility in the southeast that would get her clean. Her mother was blown away but never called me again.

Dave was another issue. Angie and I decided to take him into our home because we could not find a rehab program that would take him. He did okay for a few days. Then Micah, our son, woke in the middle of the night and saw Dave stealing from his piggy bank. When we asked Dave about it, he said it was just a mistake.

Later that morning, I took him with me to the church to mow the lawn. After a few hours, I stopped hearing the mower, but I did not think too much about it because I had given Dave a long list of chores to do. Because he had been living a homeless life for several weeks, I had also given him my "Vineyard Community of Hope" T-shirt to wear.

About this time, I got a call from the police department asking me if I was in possession of my car.

"Of course," I answered. "Why?"

"Well, there's a guy snatching purses down here at Walmart, and he seems to be driving your car and wearing one of your church T-shirts."

Sure enough, Dave had hotwired my car and stolen it. As the police pursued him, he crashed my car into a tree and totaled it. He managed to jump out of the wreckage, run away on foot and escape the police. He was eventually tracked down and thrown in jail.

We were able to help Dave find a good lawyer, but his record was so thick they said he would be put away for years. After his hearing, the judge gave him six months' hard time with no early release.

When I took Dave to jail to drop him off, I said, "I'll come back to bring you home in ninety days."

He laughed. "Didn't you hear him say hard time?"

"Yes, I did," I said. "But I'll be back in ninety days."

Some 89 days later, I got a call that Dave was being released the next day. I went to pick him up, and we drove to the Walmart parking lot, where I made him help me pray for people. In this way, we made Satan pay for all the damage he did to us and other people while Dave was under his control.

Here is how it works. If someone in my family gets sick, we pray for them to be healed, but then we also go somewhere like the hospital and pray for people there to be healed. We do this to make Satan pay for attacking us. We call it "taking a toll." Our deal with the enemy is, "If you touch one of us, you pay with three of yours. You can't cross our territory without it costing you." It works—try it!

The last I heard, Dave and Steph are doing well and living for Jesus. The car was never replaced, but I have had many other cars stolen by people in my church over the years. I have made Luci pay many tolls for them. Maybe you will help me exact more of those tolls after reading this book.

The Thief Comes to Kill

One year during our time in Aurora, we lost three church members to suicide. It was a time of tremendous heartbreak and sorrow. Angie and I had worked so hard to help them each get off drugs and to set their feet on the right path in life, and then we lost them.

After one of the suicides, I sat with one of the family members, and she made the comment, "Well, I don't understand why the Lord decided to take him home." I thought, *What? This was not God coming to take someone home. This was a person who gave up on himself and took his own life.* He had given in to the attacks of the Identity Thief, who told him he was worthless and that life was not worth living. Such terrible things happen when we allow the Thief to do what he loves to do—steal, kill and destroy.

So much of our thinking as believers has to be altered on this point. We often conclude when bad things happen that God is taking from us instead of seeing God has given everything to us. He wants us to experience life to its fullest.

Even so, I do not deny that sometimes I would get discouraged by hearing yet another person had died. I would get down on all the brokenness in our community. But then, in the middle of that sadness, another person would flee their chains and step into their true identity. Just when hope felt far away, a fresh wind of God's presence would sweep through the church, helping us stand yet again with our heads held high, rooted in the confidence that God sustains us with His power and presence. We became expectant of the freedom Christ released through us to others.

Yes, we could see we were in an uphill battle with our ministry. The Identity Thief was working overtime to steal people's very lives. But we knew our church and the other churches in the area were the solution. We were committed to prayer and breakthrough, no matter what.

During our time in Aurora, we also began to see the fruit of the Moses dream in our lives. Young people who had belonged to youth groups we had led over the years began to get in touch, sharing they had gone into ministry, become missionaries or become successful enough to provide for ministry being done around the world. In the midst of our hardship, here was more evidence of chains rattling and stones being rolled away. Amidst the death and destruction of the Identity Thief, life and hope rose up again and again.

So you see, God was not taking people home after all. It turns out He was bringing people back to life faster than the Identity Thief could take them out. And He wants to do the same in you and through you today. Arise!

13

YOU CAN RAISE THE DEAD

"Heal the sick, raise the dead, cleanse those who have leprosy, drive out demons. Freely you have received; freely give."

Matthew 10:8

The following is a report of what took place on March 9, 2015, in a small village church outside Preston, England. The event was witnessed by about eighty people in the church sanctuary. In sharing this story, I have combined the reports of four people, including myself and a medical professional. I have not included the names of the people involved because some of them were threatened after they came forward with their testimonies.

This event took place in a tight-knit village and a conservative church. I had traveled there because the pastor of the church wanted more people to learn about healing as a means of bringing people to Christ.

That evening, I had just started sharing about a DVD teaching I had for sale titled *Identity Thief* (interesting, huh?) when a woman began to shout, "My son! My son! He's having another stroke! Someone call the hospital!" She looked at me and pleaded, "Can you help him?"

I saw a strong demonic presence over the young man. His head was contorting, looking to me like it wanted to twist off. Every muscle in his body seemed strained, and he was twitching severely.

I rushed over, put my hands on the man's chest and forehead and began to bind demonic power and command the body to be loosed in Jesus' name. Many there thought he was having an epileptic seizure, but his mother told us he had never had one before. He had suffered a stroke the previous year, however.

The man started turning purple and struggling for breath.

I heard the Lord speak to me, saying, *What is about to happen, I am breaking off this entire area and nation.*

I told a few people we needed to get the man onto the ground. His body was so stiff that I felt he was less likely to injure himself on the ground than in his seat. A man standing behind us, whom I later learned was a doctor, helped move him to the ground.

Although the young man kept growing a deeper shade of purple, I could tell he had a strong, regular pulse. I asked him to tell us what he was experiencing, but his mother said, "He can't speak because of the stroke." We learned later that he had lost 95 percent of his speech ability and could say only yes and no.

As his breathing became more labored, I forbade Satan from attacking him. Meanwhile, his mother was shouting, "He's dying! My poor boy is dying!"

I still had my hand on his chest and assured her his heart was beating, but I could feel it was growing weaker as his lips turned blue and then blue-black. I could feel the spirit of death all around us. Because of this, I went from binding the spirit of infirmity to binding the spirit of death. I was nervous to say the word *death* because his distraught mother had started to shout, "He's dead!"

As I continued to break the power of the spirit of infirmity, several of us, including a medical professional, witnessed the man's pupils become fixed and dilated (as they do when people are brain dead), and his breathing became much worse. I was told this was agonal breathing, the "death rattle" that comes when people die.

Then the man stopped breathing. His head moved to the side, and saliva began running out of his mouth. I grabbed some tissue and wiped his blue-black lips and pale white cheek as I heard someone standing with me say, "He is dead."

I agreed because I could no longer feel any heartbeat.

I stepped back a second and began to recall the many prophetic words I had received about raising the dead over the years. Suddenly, all the faces of people I had prayed for in the past who had died and had not been raised began to flash before my eyes. Fear and discouragement began to creep in. The Identity Thief was fighting hard against me and this poor man.

I said, "No! No! I will not quit."

I became very angry and continued to pray more fervently. I was not willing to see this man die, and I knew other people there were praying and fighting for this poor man, as well.

I began to bind the spirit of death, saying, "You can't have him!" I also began to declare the resurrection life of Jesus

Christ over him. I stayed calm and didn't raise my voice but remained emphatic, saying, "You foul spirit of death, release him. And resurrection life of Christ, fill him now."

To my shock, the man took a deep breath!

His breathing started to recover. His eyes stopped being fixed and dilated and started to move. He blinked a few times, and color began returning to his lips and face.

We rolled him onto his side. He got on his hands and knees, but I told him to take it easy and not rush. Eventually, he was able to stand up.

He looked rather vacant at first, but as he focused on the crowd, he winked and asked, "What are they looking at?"

His mother began to shout with excitement, amazed that he could talk.

I turned toward him, pulled him into my chest—like a hug—and declared a full impartation of life. I did this because a friend of mine who has raised the dead told me, "There is something about the chest-to-chest connection that seems to impart life." When we let go, he then embraced me again.

As we helped him get to the back of the church to wait for the ambulance that was on its way, I continued to pray and break the enemy's assignment against him. The ambulance arrived shortly afterward, and the man was on his way to the hospital.

The next day, the pastor of the church called and asked if we could go to the hospital to see the young man. Upon arriving, we found out he had fractured his shoulder. They told us he needed surgery.

I asked him how he was feeling, and he said, "Pretty good, other than my shoulder." I asked if he was aware of what had happened the night before, and he said, "I know that whatever it was, it was some really bad stuff."

I told him he had died and was raised to life. He was surprised to hear it but smiled after a second or so, looking relieved, and then thanked me. The pastor verified with him that he had died.

I then asked if I could pray for his shoulder to be healed. He was very pleased to let me. We prayed, and his pain dropped from a ten down to a one. After we prayed again, he said it was at 0.5. A subsequent examination of his shoulder revealed he would not need surgery after all—surprise, surprise.

To conclude the story, I will share with you two recollections from some who witnessed the young man's resurrection:

> I can't even begin to describe to you what a terrifying moment it was to see him go and then to see God intervene in such a powerful way. If God hadn't come through, [the man] would be dead. But God showed up with a mighty display of power and love.

> I can't verify that he was "dead." I wasn't checking his pulse the whole time it was going on. But I've seen better corpses. I feel certain that he was dead and [a medical professional] concurs. So God brought him back through Robby.

We Are Meant for This

The question begs to be asked: Are we really supposed to raise the dead?

The fact of the matter is, Jesus told us to. Matthew 10:8 says, "Heal the sick, raise the dead, cleanse those who have leprosy, drive out demons." And I am of the opinion that Jesus would not have told us to do this if it was not possible.

Jesus Himself raised the dead on at least three occasions, not counting when He raised Himself from the dead. First, He raised the twelve-year-old daughter of a man named

Jairus (see Mark 5:21–43). He did this even though the people who had gathered to mourn her death laughed at him when He told them she was not dead but merely sleeping. Actually, the little girl *was* dead, but so far as the power of God is concerned, she might as well have been asleep, because God holds all power over death. And as His followers, so do we. John 3:16 assures us that anyone who believes in Jesus has eternal life—and that life begins the moment we believe.

A second account of Jesus raising a dead person is found in Luke 7:11–15:

> Soon afterward, Jesus went to a town called Nain, and his disciples and a large crowd went along with him. As he approached the town gate, a dead person was being carried out—the only son of his mother, and she was a widow. And a large crowd from the town was with her. When the Lord saw her, his heart went out to her and he said, "Don't cry."
>
> Then he went up and touched the bier they were carrying him on, and the bearers stood still. He said, "Young man, I say to you, get up!" The dead man sat up and began to talk, and Jesus gave him back to his mother.

Lastly, Jesus brought Lazarus back to life after he had been in the grave four days—dead so long, in fact, that his sister Martha told Jesus, "By this time there is a bad odor" (John 11:39).

As an aside, isn't it interesting the religious leaders plotted to kill Lazarus after his resurrection in order to destroy his testimony? John 12:10–11 says, "The chief priests made plans to kill Lazarus . . . for on account of him many of the Jews were going over to Jesus and believing in him." It should not surprise us that this was the response, though. A friend of mine who has raised a couple people from the dead warned me, "Robby, whenever you raise the dead—and you will—be prepared. Satan will try to steal that testimony. He hates the power of that testimony the most."

My friend was right. A few people who were not there the night of the man's return to life in England refuted the report of dozens of eyewitnesses, even threatening the medical professionals present and pastor for acknowledging the resurrection. I was threatened as well. My response to that has been, "There are medical professionals who testified to it, and a room full of eyewitnesses."

But back to the point at hand. We do not know for sure, but Jesus may have raised even more people from the dead. John says, "And there are also many other things which Jesus did, the which, if they should be written every one, I suppose that even the world itself could not contain the books that should be written" (John 21:25 KJV).

And then there is the testimony of what happened through the followers of Jesus. The New Testament includes two stories of resurrections that occurred after Jesus ascended into heaven. In the ninth chapter of Acts, Peter raises a woman named Tabitha, who is noted for her love and compassion for others. And Acts 20:7–12 tells a rather humorous story about a young man named Eutychus who was raised from the dead by the apostle Paul. (I say *humorous* because Eutychus died after falling from a third-story window while listening to Paul preach a particularly long-winded sermon. After going into the street and raising Eutychus from the dead, Paul then went back upstairs and continued preaching until daylight. Verse 12 says, "The people took the young man home alive and were greatly comforted." I am quite sure they were also greatly comforted by the fact that Paul's sermon had finally come to an end!)

The point I want to make is that Jesus told us to go out and heal the sick and raise the dead. If we do not do this, we are not obeying Him. It really is that simple.

Satan Seeks Our Death

Here is what we contend against, though: our enemy. Satan loves to kill and destroy. He hates humanity, and he loves to see us cry and grieve. Because of him, innocent children die because they get caught in the middle of a gang cross fire. Mothers needed by their kids lose their lives to cancer. Men with thriving ministries get cut down by drunk drivers. And so forth. I simply cannot believe such things are in agreement with God's will. This is not in keeping with what I know about God's character.

Bear in mind, though, that for the believer, death is not an enemy to be feared. I see it as a nonstop flight to paradise. Jesus told the repentant thief on the cross, "Truly I tell you, today you will be with me in paradise" (Luke 23:43), and I believe that is what happens when people of faith die. We close our eyes in this world and open them in paradise.

Death even leads to a greater existence. The apostle Paul wrote, "I desire to depart and be with Christ, which is better by far; but it is more necessary for you that I remain in the body" (Philippians 1:23–24). He also wrote, "We are confident, I say, and would prefer to be away from the body and at home with the Lord" (2 Corinthians 5:8).

For now, we cannot change the fact that everyone will die someday. Death is inevitable. But we can be the instrument God uses to bring back those who have died before their time. We can also be used to stop Satan from using death against those he steals and attacks.

We Can Pray for Their Return

When should we pray for the dead to be brought back to life? Every chance we get. I do not believe it is ever wrong to do it. Keep in mind, though, that some may not want to come back. Jesus did not bring everyone back to life. And until the fullness of the Kingdom comes, all human beings must die (see Hebrews 9:27). But we have seen there were several occasions when Jesus knew people had died before their appointed times, and He stepped in and brought them back.

Again, as we have already noted, when Jesus sent out twelve apostles, He told them, "As you go, proclaim this message: 'The kingdom of heaven has come near.' Heal the sick, raise the dead, cleanse those who have leprosy, drive out demons. Freely you have received; freely give" (Matthew 10:7–8). I believe the same charge applies to us today. Jesus said, "All authority in heaven and earth has been given to me" (Matthew 28:18). As His church, we share that authority, and that means we, too, have the power to raise the dead. Remember what Jesus said about the power we have been given:

> "Very truly I tell you, whoever believes in me will do the works I have been doing, and they will do even greater things than these, because I am going to the Father."
>
> John 14:12

God has given us the power. It is up to us to use it.

14

BE THE LIGHT IN YOUR CHURCH

"You are the light of the world. A town built on a hill cannot be hidden. Neither do people light a lamp and put it under a bowl. Instead they put it on its stand, and it gives light to everyone in the house. In the same way, let your light shine before others, that they may see your good deeds and glorify your Father in heaven."

Matthew 5:14–16

Satan loves it when he can steal the identities of Christians like you and me. But he does not stop there. He also targets churches—individual congregations and entire denominations. His wicked heart rejoices when he is able to steer a whole body of believers away from the purpose God intends for them.

Sadly, over the past few centuries, he has had some pretty good success in this area. Think of the mainline Protestant churches that lost their passion for the Gospel and began focusing on good works. Their approach became known as the "social gospel." Some of them watered down the Gospel so much that Jesus was rarely, if ever, mentioned from their pulpits. Some came to resemble Sunday morning social clubs more than the Body of Christ.

In my own career as a pastor and evangelist, I have seen congregations turn away from the life-changing, Spirit-em-powered ministry God intended for them. In some cases, the change was so abrupt that it nearly left me breathless. Revival and excitement may have been in the air, but then everything turned 180 degrees as people rejected what God was doing because, they said, "We've never done it that way before."

Jesus calls us to be salt and light in our communities. We can only do that if we know who we are—if we have resisted the Identity Thief and are standing strong as children of God. I believe we are also called to be God's light in our local congregations and our denominations. When we stand strong in our true identity, we can help our fellow believers and our churches do the same.

Caution: Identity Thief at Work

I have seen the Identity Thief at work in many movements. I have watched him move among ministers I love and care about. I have been contacted by Baptist and Methodist churches that express such pain at knowing a powerful Holy Spirit breath started their denominations and then got snuffed out, fol-lowed by denials of the power that launched them. Many of these pastors have wept on the phone with me, lamenting their history and the shift toward safe and riskless churches.

Or consider what happened with Lonnie Frisbee, whom God used so powerfully in the early '70s during the launch of both the Calvary Chapel movement and the Jesus movement. Thousands of hippies came to Christ through this young, anointed man who stood on beaches and street corners, giving a call for salvation. Multitudes responded to him. And yet when Calvary Chapel exploded in growth overnight, Lonnie was put in a back room to pray for people because too much "Holy Spirit activity" happened when he prayed—even though that was why the majority of people came to that church in the first place.

Later, in 1980, Lonnie preached on Mother's Day in John Wimber's Calvary Chapel church in Yorba Linda, California, and another movement of the Spirit was birthed. Yet the Identity Thief plotted against Lonnie a second time, not just through concealing his powerful ministry again but also by causing him to stumble in sin. As a boy, Lonnie had suffered at the hands of a child molester, which led to him battling sexual identity issues that eventually resulted in his contracting the AIDS virus and dying way too young.

Yes, the Identity Thief is at work, and not just among individual people. He goes after whole movements and seeks to take them down.

Roadblock: Vine Being Stripped Ahead

I have the most personal experience with this when it comes to the Vineyard movement, which has been my home for more than twenty years. The Identity Thief set his sights on this body of believers, too—and almost succeeded.

The birth of the Vineyard movement through Kenn Gulliksen in the 1970s, with John Wimber taking the lead in the '80s, was powerful. It came into being on the wings of what we call *power evangelism*. It marked a return to the power evident in the days of the early Church, when God confirmed His Word with signs and wonders and the Church grew rapidly around the known world.

The same happened through the Vineyard movement in those early days. Thousands around the world were impacted by John Wimber's teachings and the demonstration of healing and Holy Spirit power that flowed through him. People would come in opposition to hear him speak and end up flat on their backs, shaking from the power of God's presence. I have heard hundreds of testimonies by people impacted by John Wimber's ministry, their lives dramatically changed by it. His impact shook the world.

I love my friend Don Williams's testimony about this. He says, "When I met John Wimber, I became a Trinitarian." Beforehand, Don knew God as Father and Jesus as the Word, but he knew little of the Holy Spirit. He was a Presbyterian pastor who has since become a big part of the Vineyard movement and is a respected theologian today.

I never met John Wimber myself, but I heard him speak and minister three times. He always advocated "doing the Stuff"—meaning the supernatural, what Jesus did—and I loved his fidelity to the full implications of the Gospel.

In fact, speaking of never having met him, one time Angie and I were walking into the Anaheim Vineyard sanctuary for our first Vineyard USA conference. This was in 1997. We came around the corner, and there was John, walking toward us.

Angie said, "Quick, get the camera."

"I left it in the car," I replied.

John stopped, stared right at us and then smiled that wide-faced smile of his. We were almost afraid to move. He just stared at us for almost a full minute. Then he nodded and walked through the door.

I looked at Angie and said, "Wow. That was so cool."

As I shared in an earlier chapter, my introduction to the Vineyard movement began during the amazing stirring of God in 1994 that became dubbed "the Toronto Blessing." The Toronto Airport church, led by John and Carol Arnott, was part of the Vineyard when this revival broke out. The church began experiencing powerful visitations of the Spirit with significant healings that began to spread around the world.

However, the more prominent the Toronto Blessing became, the more it was criticized, both within and outside the Vineyard movement. John Wimber, along with many members of the Vineyard USA board, grew uncomfortable with the explanations given for the sometimes-bizarre manifestations taking place as well as the safety precautions put in place there, such as tape lines on the floor and "catchers" who stood behind people when they fell and may have encouraged the falls to happen. But the biggest issue for Wimber was his feeling there was not enough emphasis on evangelism.

The Vineyard board began to question whether the Toronto church still looked to the Vineyard for its covering, given its many connections to other streams around the world. From what I have been told by several members of the board, some of the board members wanted the matters of the Spirit toned down to better legitimize the movement.

Wimber was in poor health at this time and weary of defending the issue. He flew with a team to meet with the Arnotts to discuss the matter but did not give them a meeting agenda beforehand. The Arnotts, feeling themselves put in a difficult position of having to choose whether to stay or go, decided it was best to withdraw from the Vineyard movement altogether. Many Vineyard leaders grieved, while others celebrated. In the end, I believe the Identity Thief worked to divide these two powerful streams.

Again, this pattern has repeated itself for generations in Church history through so many denominations that start with a powerful outpouring of the Spirit. Eventually, certain factions begin to pressure leaders to tone down the Holy Spirit–driven practices. I believe this is what led Jack Hayford to deliver a powerful prophetic warning to the Vineyard movement in the late 1990s that has become well known on YouTube, where he said, "You are so vulnerable to living out what I watched and lived in. . . . It's one of the places that you decide whether you're going to live in the river or just know the map of where the river was." The Vineyard movement was in danger of being hacked.

I experienced some of this firsthand myself. It actually got to the point where, when I would get together with other Vineyard pastors and leaders at national and regional meetings, Angie would ask me not to tell stories about healings or miracles. She knew I was heartbroken every time I would hear them say, "Oh, that's old-school Vineyard. We don't do that now."

Angie would tell me, "You have incredible stories to tell. These are your trophies of what God has done through your ministry. But the people who are part of the group we're in, they don't value these things like they once did."

She was right. It would break my heart to hear this, even though I knew it was true.

But the Identity Thief would not have the final victory here. In 2010, I traveled with Vineyard pastor Ed Loughran and a few others to wash the feet of John and Carol Arnott. We were seeking their release of the Vineyard USA of anything that may have been brought upon it as a result of the parting of ways that had happened. Through our conversation, it became clear the Identity Thief had done his work on both sides of the aisle, causing confusion, trouble and theft of the greater work intended for this incredible outpouring.

The Arnotts were so gracious and humble in their response to us. John had never had his feet washed before and felt so uncomfortable with it, but he was willing to let us do it. Through tears, they blessed us and the Vineyard USA. They assured us they bore no ill will toward the movement. Then they prayed for us and, yes, once again I ended up on my back.

Now a big shift back has occurred. Millions of people all over the world have witnessed through documentary movies like *Furious Love* and *Father of Lights* the miracles that have happened. I hear Vineyard pastors worldwide say, "We are pressing into doing the Stuff once again." John Wimber gave us a legacy that we are starting again to live.

Warning: Pitfalls in the Road

When self-preservation takes over, it destroys faith. When we start to become risk averse, no longer willing to step out in faith, we lose our awe of God. An encounter with God should be both elating and terrifying. We are never going to get near almighty God without being at risk.

Our risk aversion may have something to do with being afraid God will do something weird, and we do not want Him to rock the boat. We want to stay in our comfort zone, not wanting Him to do anything that might embarrass us in front of our noncharismatic friends. One pastor said to me, "I just don't want people to get freaked out or nervous in church." I thought, *Then you may be trying to protect them from encountering God.*

God can be freaky sometimes. Thinking our job is to protect people from God is a thought that only comes from one source: Satan, the Identity Thief.

I think of a young woman who attended our church. She told me, "My boyfriend's coming to church with me, and I really hope he becomes a Christian. But he's one of these people, if anything weird happens, he'll get up and run."

Well, as God would have it, near the end of the service the boyfriend attended, a couple people went under the power of the Spirit. They fell to the floor and started shaking as if electrocuted—right in front of the boyfriend.

I saw his eyes grow big and knew he was probably terrified. So I stepped over, put my hand on his shoulder and asked, "Do you know what you're seeing here?"

He thought a moment and answered, "Well, I think if God came upon a human being, this is kind of what it would look like."

"Are you afraid of this?" I asked.

"Part of me is," he said. "But part of me wants it."

I said, "Yeah, that's how God works."

The boyfriend did not run out of the church at all. He wound up giving his life to Christ and becoming a faithful, active member of the congregation. So you see, when we step aside and let God do what He wants to do, amazing things happen.

Think about some of the risks the apostles took. Jesus told them to feed five thousand people with a few loaves and fishes (see Mark 6:30–44).

It all began when the disciples came to Jesus and said, "Uh, we've got a problem. We've got a lot of hungry people here, and we don't have anything to feed them."

They even had a solution.

"We've been thinking about it, Lord," they said, "and we think You can send them away while there's still time for them to make it into town before the restaurants close."

In other words, they were saying, "Lord, we've already come up with a plan. All we need is for You to make it work."

Instead, Jesus said, "You feed them."

Can you just imagine their reaction? It was probably something along the lines of, "Say what? Ha ha. Sorry, Jesus, but it sounded for a minute like You said, 'You feed them.'"

"I did," He responded.

"With what?"

Jesus smiled and asked, "What have you got?"

So they brought Him a little boy with a few small loaves of bread and some fish.

"That will do," He said.

I am sure they were thinking, *It won't do, Lord! We're going to look like fools if we try to feed this huge crowd with this tiny bit of food.* In my mind's eye, I can see the disciples going into the crowd, each with a handful of crumbs, saying to the people, "I know this is crazy, but this is what Jesus told us to do. Please, just go along with it. Just take a little bit, okay?"

Except the more they gave, the more bread and fish there was.

I doubt the disciples even knew a miracle had taken place until the teenagers in the crowd started having a food fight. I can picture them acting like kids everywhere do, throwing bits of bread and fish at each other because they were full. Meantime, the disciples were still passing out small handfuls of food.

The message here is this: If we will give Jesus what we have, He will multiply it.

And what about that little boy? He went home with twelve baskets full of food that day. If he had lived on the east side of Aurora, Illinois, where I planted my church, his mother would have been hollering at him, asking, "Where did you steal that?"

The point is that Jesus shows us what happens when we surrender to Him. When we put our identity into His hands, even when doing so does not make sense, He multiplies the work. He can do so much more through us if we abandon our comfort zone and let Him move with power.

He can even overcome the work of the Identity Thief against whole groups of people if we let Him, as we have seen in this chapter. Some give up on their associations, denominations and movements due to the discouraging work of the enemy. They separate because they no longer see the Spirit at work in the way He once was among their ranks. Others stay, tempered from trailblazing pioneers into placid homesteaders.[1] These two dynamics have been at odds within the Church since its beginning days.

We should never forget, though, that there remains a remnant God will honor. He does not give up on anyone. He can reignite the light in a place through us if we stay true to what we know is His work and do not yield our identity to the work of the Identity Thief. I believe total breakthrough will come.

15

WHO ARE YOU?

The Spirit himself testifies with our spirit that we are God's children. Now if we are children, then we are heirs—heirs of God and co-heirs with Christ, if indeed we share in his sufferings in order that we may also share in his glory.

Romans 8:16–17

The nineteenth chapter of Acts tells the story of seven sons of a Jewish chief priest named Sceva who were trying to cast out demons "in the name of the Jesus whom Paul preaches" (verse 13). They did this even though they did not know Jesus personally. They did not belong to Him. Even so, they knew there was power in His name, so they used it. But then:

One day the evil spirit answered them, "Jesus I know, and Paul I know about, but who are you?" Then the man who had the evil spirit jumped on them and overpowered them all. He gave them such a beating that they ran out of the house naked and bleeding.

Acts 19:15–16

It is kind of a funny story.

The main point is that these seven young men did not have the wisdom to use the name of Jesus because they did not have a relationship with Him. As far as we know, they were just tinkering with authority rather than walking in their true identity. They had no right to wear His identity (just like David could not wear the armor of Saul; see 1 Samuel 17:38–39), because they were not in relationship with Jesus. Paul and the other apostles were able to cast out demons and perform many other miracles because they *were* identified with Christ.

If you have given your life to Him, then you are part of His family, and, like Paul and the other apostles, you have the right to use His name and authority.

You Have the Power

It does not matter whether you are young or old, weak or strong, male or female, tall or short, black or white, or any other thing. If you belong to Jesus, He has given you the power and authority to heal the sick, raise the dead, cast out demons and perform other signs and wonders in His name.

Let me give you another example to show this is true. Earlier this year, I was in Asheville, North Carolina, for Youth-Quake 2015, an event hosted by Vineyard, Bethel and Anglican churches. I look forward to this event every year because God always meets us there, and many healings take place. I also love being a part of these three streams flowing together.

This year was no exception.

One of my favorite moments came when I asked a young lady named Amberlee to pray for a young man with a shoulder injury. Amberlee had just accepted Jesus the previous evening, and the Lord showed His love for her by healing her shoulder. Now she was stepping out in faith, taking a risk to pray for the healing of another, something she had never done before.

As she finished praying, the boy's face lit up and he said, "The pain is gone!"

He then asked me, "Would you please pray for my leg to grow out? My hip is degenerating, and it is one and a quarter inches too short now."

I asked Amberlee to pray for him again, and as she did, his leg grew in plain sight of us all—and in front of cameras that caught it all on video. I was brought to tears by the joy on the faces of this young man and the girl who had stepped out in faith to pray for him. Amberlee took a gigantic leap of faith, and God caught her. She was seeing her true identity. And the very next month, that fifteen-year-old boy ran a marathon and came in second—to a 25-year-old marine!

All God wants and needs are willing hands and hearts.

Be Fearless

I have seen firsthand the devastation AIDS has caused through a visit I took to Africa. An amazing woman whose husband was brutally murdered for preaching the Gospel invited me to come to that nation to minister. She did not understand why God had taken her husband home, she told me, but she was just trusting Him. I replied, "Your husband was martyred for the sake of the Gospel. Satan came to kill him."

Even though my schedule was completely full, Angie and I decided I should agree to go. My goal was to win hundreds of souls for Christ—to exact a toll on Satan for what he had done to this man of God.

I want to share the story of this trip with you because of the many moments Satan tried to implant fear into my heart and the hearts of others who were with us. I want to show you that we cannot live in fear of the Identity Thief or let him steal the show. God wants to move powerfully through us to take people back from the Thief and demonstrate His glory through them as they learn to walk in their true identity. Fear cannot hold us back.

We made the trip in June 2013, along with two fellow Vineyard pastors who were also good friends, Barry Long and Van Cochrane. We had two weeks filled with training on power evangelism, then hit the streets and put it all into action for the churches there.

The trip culminated at an open-air meeting. We were exhausted but invigorated by the transformation that would occur at this location.

Hundreds of people came together, most of them among the poorest I had ever seen. They were ragged, hungry and in need of Jesus. Many of them were suffering from HIV and AIDS.

My personal ministry team consisted of the two adult children of the man of God who had been murdered. Tears filled their eyes as they prayed with me for healing and led many to Christ. That ministry, I told them, was our great revenge against Satan.

And Christ demonstrated Himself as a righteous judge as we saw His presence rise in that place. More than two hundred people surrendered to Him, and there were so many healings it was not possible to give an accurate count. AIDS is no match for the love and power of Jesus. God's revenge was in full swing.

Remember, this is the upside-down Kingdom. And so it was that one of the first people to accept Jesus was a well-known prostitute in the area. I showed her how she could pray for others and see them healed, too.

At first some of the pastors were not happy with this. They knew the woman's reputation. But I told them this is exactly how God demonstrates His power—He uses the people Satan once had in his grip, someone the Identity Thief had made to feel worthless. This woman's false identity was *prostitute*. Her true identity was *righteous princess*. What a joy it was to see her embrace and accept her true identity!

Halfway through that trip to Africa, we were in a city about two hours away from Zimbabwe's capital city of Harare. In each city we visited, we would go to the marketplace during the day to do healings and give prophetic words. By evening, word would have spread so fast that God was healing people and speaking to people that our evening service would fill to overflowing.

On this particular day, our host showed me a letter he had received from the local police chief. It said that if we continued to meet in the market area and hold open-air meetings, they would "arrest us," "beat us" and "extradite us."

The pastor said, "Robby, you need to weigh this seriously, because they will do it."

I said, "I don't doubt that they will, but we are seeing so much happening that we might as well continue."

The following day, I was told by my host that the threat now extended not just to me and my team but to every pastor in the entire city. This was a game changer, as I did not feel it appropriate to make the decision to leave or stay on behalf of every pastor in the city.

Our host told me he felt I was viewed as the real threat in the situation and that they could send me back to Harare but continue the evening meetings with the rest of my team. I agreed, but before we left the city, I had my driver pull off at a gas station so I could jump out and pray for some people there who needed healing. As soon as we were back on the road, a police car zipped up behind us and, with lights flashing, pulled us over.

The officer came to the window and told us we were in violation of the law, as we had been asked to leave. He took our papers, went back to his car for about fifteen minutes—and then came and told us we were free to go, as he could not get his police chief on the radio for some reason.

Once again, God had intervened on our behalf!

Upon returning to Harare, Darrin, the pastor of the Vineyard church there, met us and told me, "Robby, what happened to you is why I am afraid to pray for people publicly. I don't mind praying for them in their homes or in my church, but praying for them out in the open has always terrified me."

I told Darrin that if he would come with me to the marketplace, I would show him how he could get over that fear. The next day, we went with a few others to an open area where hundreds of people gathered for public transportation.

I turned to Darrin and said, "Stick right beside me. Do exactly as I say, and I promise you'll never be afraid to do this again."

Darrin was under the impression he was only going to have to stand and watch me minister and that this would eliminate his fear. I told him, "Darrin, you are not a fearful person. The fear that you feel is a lie from the enemy. You must trust who God says you are."

As we jumped out of the van, I turned to Darrin and said, "Are you with me?"

"Yes, I'm ready to watch," he answered.

I then turned to the crowd and shouted, "Anybody who needs healing, come over here now. My friend Darrin will pray for you, and Jesus will heal you."

Darrin looked at me in utter shock and horror as dozens of people began to surround him. There was no way out but to pray.

After about thirty minutes of praying, Darrin called to me, "Robby, look!"

He held out his hand, and I could see it was calm and still.

"No fear!" he exclaimed.

After leaving Zimbabwe, I received an email from several people telling me I had ruined Darrin. All he wanted to do anymore was go into public places to do healing and give prophetic words that would bring people to Jesus. He was no longer hacked by the Identity Thief. He was living his true identity.

Do you see all that happened on this trip because fear was not given a foothold? We drew near to those with disease because we knew God wanted to heal them. We believed God wanted to exact a toll from Satan for the death of Pam's husband, so we walked boldly into the place where his killer might have been. We spoke truth when other believers wanted to diminish the work of freedom God was bringing to His children. We kept up our ministry even when threatened by authorities. We trusted God would reign supreme. And we helped others embrace a life of freedom from fear, which God turned into increased ministry power through them.

This is the life God means for you to have. Will you let Him give it to you?

Heal People

If you only open your eyes and look, you will see there are battles to be fought everywhere—and we can be used to gain the victory. What is more, we *need* to be used. If not us, then who?

For instance, I was sitting beside a lady on a flight to China one time when I noticed she had a brace on her arm and her fingers were curled up. She was throwing back drinks, so I knew she was in pain.

"What's wrong with your arm?" I asked.

"Oh, I work in downtown Chicago," she said, "and I slipped on the ice and hurt my hand. I've had three surgeries and have been through physical therapy, but it doesn't seem to get better."

"Are you in pain?" I asked.

"Yes. It's really hurting bad."

"Well, we can pray for that," I said. "All of the pain can go away right now. Jesus really loves you. He's in pursuit of a relationship with you."

"Well, I'm not really a churchbody."

I laughed. "Well, I'm not sure what a churchbody is, but this is about a relationship."

She allowed me to pray for the pain to go away, and it did—instantly. Then I prayed for the numbness to leave and for the feeling to come back.

She kept looking at her hand like my baby boy looked at his hand, mesmerized. She reached into her handbag, grabbed a ball and squeezed it. As she did, a tear rolled down her cheek.

"I've never been able to do that before," she said.

That same day, on my connecting flight, I was just getting comfortable in my seat when a message came over the PA system.

"We have a medical emergency," the flight attendant said. "Is there a doctor on board?"

I got up and headed toward the section of the plane where the emergency was and found a little girl in distress. She was about three years old and had a temperature of 104. Another gentleman was there to help. He was a pediatrician, and he asked the flight attendant for some ice packs to help bring the girl's fever down.

I asked if I could pray for her.

The pediatrician said, "Look, this is a medical emergency. Let me handle it."

When he went to get the ice packs, I told the girl's mom I could pray for her daughter right then and she could be healed.

"Do it," she said.

The doctor was upset when he came back and saw me praying for the girl, and the flight attendant ordered me back to my seat. But when they took the child's temperature again, it had fallen to 101.

When we reached our destination, the flight attendant thanked me for praying and told me the little girl was doing just fine with a temperature of 98.

"We didn't even have to give her any medicine," she said, smiling.

Now, why didn't that surprise me?

Change Worlds

Never forget who you are in Christ. If you have thoughts or feelings that make you feel bad about yourself, remember they come from the enemy. Do not believe Satan's lies. You are not who he says you are.

The thoughts and feelings he throws on you do not define who you are, either. For example, having a lustful thought does not mean you are a lustful person. You have no reason to be ashamed of yourself.

Satan cannot read your mind, but he can put thoughts and feelings on you. The only way he knows he has made a hit is by watching what you say and do. If he puts a lustful thought in your mind, for instance, and you say, *Oh, I'm such a lustful person*, he laughs and says, *I've got him*.

The Bible says Jesus was tempted in every way we are tempted. This means even He must have been tempted to lust, but He refused to give in to it. He turned it around and defeated those things. They could not hold sway over Him.

That is the response I try to have, too. If I see an attractive woman while I am driving down the road, for example, and am tempted to lust, I turn Satan's curse into a blessing. I pray, *Lord, bless that woman. Bring her into a right relationship with You. I thank You that You're going to use her to do great things for Your Kingdom.* I even roll my window down and start telling that woman Jesus is going to use her to change her community by bringing loads of people to Christ.

When Satan hears this, he screams, *Cease-fire! Retreat!* He knows I am turning his darts back on him.

The enemy is always trying to confuse us, manipulate us and make us think we are not who we really are. People often tell me, "I wish I could do what you do, but I'm just not that courageous." That is a lie from Satan. That is how he wants you to see yourself—as lacking courage. Or someone tells me, "I'm just a selfish person." That, too, is a lie from the enemy. When the enemy tells you these things about yourself, just tell him, *That's a lie, and I reject it in the name of Jesus.* Never listen to Satan's lies.

The truth is, you are meant to change whole worlds. Do you know how that happens? One person at a time.

One time, when I was a guest speaker in a church, God gave me a word for a young man who was sitting in the audience. I pointed at him and said, "The Lord is showing me that you've had a lot of struggles in your family."

Before I could continue, the young man stood up and started running in place. Then he turned and ran for the door. When the youth pastor stepped in front of him and tried to stop him, the young man began shouting, "I've got to get out of here! I've got to get out of here!"

I bound the spirit of fear in prayer, and the young man's shoulders dropped and his panic subsided.

"God wants you to know He has His hand on your life," I said.

I continued giving him a prophetic word from the Lord, and he dropped his head and began to weep.

A year and a half later, when I was back in that church, I got to hear the end of that story when I saw the young man again. He said, "I've got to tell you how that changed my life. Before that, I had one foot in the church and one in the world. But when you called me, I heard this voice say, *You've got to get out of here. He's going to reveal all your sins.* I was panicked. It was like the church was on fire. But when you began to pray for me, the voice stopped and I felt fine. And everything you said to me has come to pass."

Again, you do not have to listen to Satan—ever. There is no catch. The power is yours. You just have to step out in faith and use it.

You do not have to be perfect. (Besides, if you belong to Jesus, you already are perfect because you are covered by His righteousness.) You do not have to spend years in the desert, learning how to be a channel of God's power and practicing it. You do not have to learn how to pray long, eloquent prayers that move everyone who hears you to tears. You do not have to fix anything first. Jesus already did. You do not have to become anything special first. The special One already lives in you.

Jesus is already at work all around you every day and is inviting you to participate. Just dive headfirst into the Jesus life. Have faith in Him. Step out in His power. God can and will use you to do what Jesus did.

Live your true identity as a world changer!

NOTES

Chapter 1: We've Been Hacked!

1. Javelin Strategy and Research, "More Than Twelve Million Identity Fraud Victims in 2012 According to Latest Javelin Strategy and Research Report," February 20, 2013, https://www.javelinstrategy.com/news/1387/92/More-Than-12-Million-Identity-Fraud-Victims-in-2012-According-to-Latest-Javelin-Strategy-Research-Report/d,pressRoomDetail.

2. TransUnion, "Identity Theft Facts," http://www.transunion.com/personal-credit/identity-theft-and-fraud/identity-theft-facts.page.

3. Chad Terhune, "Anthem Hack Exposes Data on Eighty Million; Experts Warn of Identity Theft," *Los Angeles Times*, February 5, 2015, http://www.latimes.com/business/la-fi-anthem-hacked-20150204-story.html#page=1.

Chapter 3: God Uses Wounded Warriors

1. I am grateful for the contribution my dear friend Nicole Voelkel made to this chapter by providing me with her personal eyewitness account of the events we experienced in the Dominican Republic.

Chapter 5: Stay Plugged In

1. Daniel Goleman, "Long-Married Couples Do Look Alike, Study Finds," *New York Times*, August 11, 1987, http://www.nytimes.com/1987/08/11/science/long-married-couples-do-look-alike-study-finds.html.

Chapter 9: Know Who You Are

1. John Wimber and Kevin Springer, *Power Healing* (New York: Harper Collins, 1987).

Chapter 10: Receive a New Heart

1. Robby Dawkins, *Do What Jesus Did* (Bloomington, MN: Chosen, 2013), 48. For the full story, see pages 43–48.

Chapter 14: Be the Light in Your Church

1. I thank my friend Tri Robinson for first providing me with this image of pioneers and homesteaders through an article he wrote on his blog, www.trirobinson.org.

Robby Dawkins and his wife, Angie, have been married 23 years and have six sons. Robby is a fifth-generation pastor born to missionary parents in Japan. He served as a youth pastor for twelve years before planting a Vineyard church in downtown Aurora, Illinois, where 70 percent of members came to Christ at the church and 60 percent were saved through power encounters. In 2013, the mayor of Aurora, along with its chief of police, bestowed upon Robby and his church an acknowledgment that he and the church had made a significant difference in Aurora's crime-rate reduction. Robby and Angie served the Aurora church from 1996–2013.

Today, Robby travels extensively as an itinerant minister, crossing denominational and nondenominational lines to equip churches in power evangelism. He has spoken in 46 countries and to audiences of more than eleven thousand people. Most recently, he was featured in the movies *Furious Love* (2010), *Father of Lights* (2012) and *Holy Ghost: Reborn* (2015). He has been featured on GOD TV, TBN and Sid Roth's *It's Supernatural!* His book *Do What Jesus Did*, released in 2013, has ranked on three of Amazon's bestseller lists and has met with success in the United States, the United Kingdom and Europe.

For more information, visit www.robbydawkins.com. Connect with Robby on Facebook at www.facebook.com /robbydawkinsministries or on Twitter at www.twitter.com /robbydawkins.

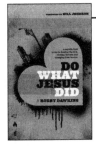